Hungarian Vizsla

Or Magyar Vizsla Dog

Hungarian Vizsla Complete Dog Manual

Hungarian Vizsla dog care, costs, feeding, grooming, health and training all included.

by

Matthew Burston

Disclaimer

The Author has strived to be as accurate and complete as possible in the creation of this book, notwithstanding the fact that he does not warrant or represent at any time that the contents within are accurate due to the rapidly changing nature of the subject.

While all attempts have been made to verify information provided in this publication, the Author assumes no responsibility for errors, omissions, or contrary interpretation of the subject matter herein.

Table of Contents

Table of Contents

Foreword

Are you looking for a dog companion that can add splendor to your life? Searching for a pick-me-up-when-I-am-down? When it comes to dogs, you have over 150 different dog breeds to choose from. So what really sets each of them apart?

It is this: each dog breed has unique characteristics. Ranging from their physical appearance down to their personality traits – each dog breed is infinitely different from another.

So while you can pick and choose just about any dog breed, matching it with your own personality and lifestyle ensures you'll be able to spend a memorable time with your pet.

The dog breed in general is known for its loyalty and protective behavior. Proper training can further enhance their positive behaviors and limit the negative ones. So your pet truly becomes your shadow!

Here you will find everything you need to know about the Hungarian Vizsla breed – how to take care of it, how and what to feed it, how to go about its grooming and training concerns, and everything pertaining to this outclass breed.

Read through carefully before you decide to bring your canine companion home.

Chapter 1: Introduction

Dogs make loyal companions – there is no doubt about it. It is the distinctive personality traits that each dog breed possesses which makes each one attractive in a different manner to different people.

When it comes to the number of dog breeds known to us, a mounting figure of more than 150 comes up. However, according to their personalities, they can be broadly categorized into 7 groups.

1. Sporting Group
2. Hound Group
3. Working Group
4. Terrier Group
5. Toy Group
6. Non-Sporting Group
7. Herding Group

There are a few other breeds which are readily gaining recognition by dog clubs all over the world. They are currently classified as miscellaneous group because their personality traits have not yet been generalized.

The dog breed discussed here is the Hungarian Vizsla, also known as the Magyar Vizsla dog. Naturally, the breed is native to the country of Hungary. It receives its name from the Hungarian definition of the word "Vizsla" which means "alert and responsive".

The Hungarian Vizsla is categorized under the sporting group due to its nature. According to its size, it is considered to be a medium sized dog breed. This makes the Hungarian Vizsla ideal for almost all aspiring dog owners.

In general, it is easier to take care of a Hungarian Vizsla but like every other dog breed, there are a few things you need to be careful about while living with this dog breed. This book will give you an insight about everything that you need to know.

The Hungarian Vizsla generally has a skinny appearance. The absence of hair on its body further highlights the dog's muscles and structure. It may look malnourished in the first look. This is why it is important for you to know what a happy and healthy Hungarian Vizsla looks like before you head off to purchase one!

Before you get influenced by the impulse of purchasing a Hungarian Vizsla or any other dog breed for that matter, it is important for you to understand that this is not about a short-term association. Most dogs live up to a decade or more. If you are not up for such a responsibility, it is better not to head this way!

Ask yourself; do you really want a Hungarian Vizsla dog or are you possibly looking for a small sized toy dog? Are there other dog breeds that you find more exciting than the Hungarian Vizsla? Know what you really want before you actually go through the trouble of purchasing one!

And if you are worried about how, from where, and for how much should you buy a Hungarian Vizsla, fret not! This book contains answers to all your questions!

In addition to this, we have included detailed information about how to care for this breed, how to train it and how to make it people-friendly to adjust with your lifestyle.

Everything you need to know about this breed is contained here. Keep reading to find out if Hungarian Vizsla is really the dog you are looking for. And once you've made the decision to buy, get one immediately!

Chapter 2: The Hungarian Vizsla – The Alert and Responsive Breed

The Hungarian Vizsla is unique in every sense. From its looks to its habits and personality, you would probably not find any other dog breed that comes even close to this particular one.

So if you are planning to get one, it is important for you to understand its specific needs beforehand. Prior experience of handling dogs can prepare you for the task. But even then, you'll need to devote some time to comprehend this breed before you can help it blend in with your lifestyle.

Here are a few facts about the Hungarian Vizsla breed that will not only prove to be informative for you, but will also serve as light entertainment before the real story!

1) Some Facts about the Hungarian Vizsla Breed

The Hungarian Vizsla usually looks a little malnourished for two reasons; its skin stretches tightly over its muscles and it doesn't have a lot of hair to cover it up. But when you contrast it against the kind of energy and hyperactivity it displays, you'll understand why it is considered as one of the challenging dog breeds.

Here are a few fun facts to get you started with this amazing dog breed.

1. The Hungarian Vizsla is more than 1000 years old! The early artworks made by renowned artists several hundreds of years ago contain images of this dog breed – a sure indication of the fact that this dog breed existed back then. It has not only survived through these years but has also thrived tremendously in the region!

2. The Hungarian Vizsla is particularly popular in Hungary, so much so that it was given the status of being an aristocratic symbol for royals. In this part of the world, the Hungarian Vizsla is the singularly most popular dog breed for people.
3. During the Russian colonization of Hungary in the year 1945, attempts were made to eradicate this dog breed from the region. As it was a symbol of royalty, the Russians tried to stamp them out to symbolize the occupancy of Hungary. The dog breed survived due to those few dog enthusiasts who smuggled their beloved companions out of the country.
4. The Hungarian Vizsla is one of the oldest dog breeds to be recognized by almost all dog clubs around the world. The American Kennel Club recognized the breed in 1960!
5. The Hungarian Vizsla is said to be "self-colored". It has a distinctive golden rustic color on its body. Even the nose, nails and eye lids are of more or less the same color. In fact, any evident black or white patches on the Vizsla can disqualify it from its breed.
6. It is ranked as the 54th most popular dog breed in the world.
7. The Vizslas are extremely people oriented. They crave for the human touch and can go to any length in order to achieve it. If you try to lock them up in secluded rooms or you try to kennel train them, they will try their best to escape from this captivity. They like being free, being loved and being in touch with their human masters!
8. The Vizsla is a self-cleaner – a trait it seems to have adopted from its distant four-legged cousins called cats! So if you are the kind of person who wants a clean dog without much effort, the Hungarian Vizsla can be your first choice!
9. The Hungarian Vizslas are sometimes referred to as the "Velcro" dog breed. This signifies their love for their human masters.
10. The Hungarian Vizsla does not have an undercoat unlike most other dog breeds. It cannot survive out in the cold. So you need to be extra careful about keeping it adequately warm indoors during the winter months.

11. The Hungarian Vizsla's sense of smell is spectacular. This is one reason why these are often referred to as the pointers. They've been used for hunting purposes previously. Since the decline in hunting activities, the Hungarian Vizsla has transformed into a companion dog.

The Hungarian Vizsla possesses an illustrative history. There are still a few disagreements about where and how the breed originated. Migration of people all over the world has contributed towards its gene pool.

Nevertheless, it was not until the 19th century that the Hungarian Vizsla was officially recognized. It took another couple of years for the dog clubs to produce general guidelines for this breed.

Here is a little insight about how the Hungarian Vizsla came into being.

2) A Brief History of Hungarian Vizsla

The earliest records of the Hungarian Vizsla can be dated back to the 11th century. A few artworks contain evident "statements" that talk about the presence of this breed. So we can safely assume this dog breed has survived through a couple of centuries!

In the 14th and 15th century, the Hungarian Vizsla was documented as a hunter because of its spectacular sense of smell. They were used to hunt down Pheasants, Quails and Grouses. Its lean and sprightly structure coupled with its hunting capabilities contributed towards its role. However, over time, as the hunting activities were discouraged globally for ecological reasons, the Hungarian Vizsla was lost to this purpose.

The Hungarian Vizsla is still used for hunting small fur animals and Waterfowl though such activities are fairly limited. The Hungarian Vizsla has become more of a companion dog than a hunting dog.

Chapter 2: The Hungarian Vizsla – The Alert and Responsive Breed

---

During the middle of 16th century, Turkey occupied Hungary and established it as an extension of the Ottoman Empire. The occupancy continued over a period of more than one and a half century. During this time, it is believed that the Hungarian Vizsla was crossbred with the Turkish Quail-hunting dogs. This aims to explain the dog's rustic brown coat. Even so, there is no scientific evidence to support such a claim.

Then on, the Hungarian Vizsla breed was cross bred with the German short haired pointer breed, the English pointer breed and the blood hounds. This resulted in the formation of the present day characteristics of the Hungarian Vizsla breed.

The Hungarian Vizsla possesses pointer characteristics. Whenever the Vizsla senses the bait, it goes rigid in the body and points out the direction with its nose. This is how it used to signal hunters about prospective hunting animals in the vicinity. It still possesses these characteristics, more so due to the cross breeding with pointer breeds from different origins.

The Hungarian Vizsla as we know now has received its personality from several dog breeds. It coat distinctively provides evidence of the fact that it has its roots in the Turkish Quail hunting dog breeds. At the same time, its pointer capabilities provide evidence for the fact that it was once crossed with hunter breeds. This has greatly revolutionized its role in the contemporary world.

During the occupations of Hungary, the Vizsla consistently became the target of conquests. It is believed that during the World War II, the Hungarian Vizsla was almost entirely lost to the battles. Only a few of this breed survived which then became the propagators of this breed.

This adequately summarizes the history of the Hungarian Vizsla. This explains a lot about this breed. To find out more, keep reading!

Chapter 3: Breeding

Today, the Hungarian Vizsla cannot really be regarded as an endangered breed, nor is it one of those that have limited availability. Regardless of where you live, you will be able to find a reputable Hungarian Vizsla breeder in your vicinity – preferably recognized by the local kennel club.

The most important part about this is to ensure the dog was bred professionally. For the Hungarian Vizsla, breeding makes all the difference between a long-lived healthy dog and the one which is prone to a number of health and hereditary problems. Here are a few pointers you should keep in mind while selecting your breeder and your dog.

1) Establishing a Reputable Breeder

First and foremost, before you move forward with your pet acquisition, take your time you establish a reputable breeder. It is the breeder which makes all the difference for your relationship with your pet. Here are a few considerations you should keep in mind.

Firstly, it is important for you to understand why every person cannot be a breeder. There are a lot of intricacies involved in the breeding process which the professional ones take care of. But if an inexperienced breeder tries to do the same, the results may not be as “acceptable” to you.

There are over 150 different dog breeds present in this world. Previously, due to inadequate education and awareness, cross breeding was pretty common. When dogs from different breeds mate, the resulting litter possesses characteristics from both parents, which makes it difficult to categorize them under any particular head.

Another major downside to cross breeding is that it promotes several hereditary problems. It has actually given rise to a number of health complications in dogs. It has polluted the dog gene pool to an extent that almost all breeds have developed significant challenges in terms of health.

This is why an emphasis is placed on pure breeding or pure bred dogs for adoption. This does not only ensure your dog exhibits the right characteristics but also that it will probably live healthier and longer.

As a dog enthusiast, a proud owner of the Hungarian Vizsla or even as someone observing the situation through a critical lens, losing a beloved pet to fate is the last thing you want. While you cannot really deny the facts, you can surely delay the imminent for as long as possible!

The most evident factor that can help you determine the authenticity of the breeder is this; the professional breeders usually put their specimen through extensive medical testing procedures to ensure that they are absolutely healthy and fit for mating.

The screening procedure aims to qualify the dog across all measures. The specimen will be tested for known medical problems as well as those that are likely to occur in the given breed. The specimen is put through a 360degree scrutiny to ensure the litter has the least probability of contracting any problems.

The best breeder – or the one who knows s/he is doing it rightly – will obtain these certifications from reputed dog clubs in the region. For instance, in the United States, the American Kennel Club is the most popular destination for dog certifications. This club puts the specimen through robust screening procedures. Their document is considered valuable across the globe.

The thing about AKC certification is that they authorize pure breeds only. This further adds value to the certificate and ensures your dog possesses the right set of characteristics. A pedigree is always considered more valuable than other dogs.

There are other certifying agencies that will be more than willing to issue their certificates on a single call. Their reliability is considered questionable for the very reason that such organizations often will not undertake any effort to find out whether the dog is a purebred healthy one or not.

So if you've located a reputable breeder in your vicinity, you are done with the most tedious task. Rest assured, the breeder can make a lot of difference.

Another way to look for individual dog breeders is to ask the reputed clubs. In most cases, national will be able to provide you a detailed list of reputable breeders in the vicinity that are affiliated with them.

Since the list is provided by the dog club itself, it is almost implied that the dog club endorses these individual breeders for their professional breeding activities. This also adds authenticity to the breeder's offering.

There are a number of breeders that you will be able to access online. The thing about them is that they can fool you quite easily. So you need to make an extra effort to ensure the online dog breeder is genuine.

For the most part, don't rely on anything that you do not see with your own eyes or cannot feel with your hands. But if you are still hoping to trust an online breeder, make sure you ask for references.

Visit the customers as well as the breeder's facility if possible. Take your time to establish whether it is really a genuine case or not. Only then you should begin thinking about actually acquiring a pet.

On a similar note, customer references can also help you greatly with your feat. If there is someone you know who is already in possession of a Hungarian Vizsla, you can ask him/her where they got it from and how it has been. If you find satisfactory answers, you've got all the more reason to pursue your companionship in the same way as the other person did!

2) Meeting its Parents

It is generally recommended for you to see not only the puppy that you are about to purchase but also its parents before making your decision. Looking at the parents can help put a lot of your concerns at ease.

For instance, looking at the parents can help you figure out whether they are healthy or not. Healthy kids are usually born to healthy parents so you can naturally make out the logic in this sequence of events.

Even if you are not able to meet the parents properly, you should at least ask for their pictures and medical certificates. The picture alone can suffice where you cannot meet the parents in person.

Additionally, most experts and conditioned dog enthusiasts admit having records about the dog's aunts and uncles can also serve as an eye opener. Even though they are not essential for making decisions, it nevertheless helps you get a good idea about what you are getting yourself into.

It is highly recommended for you to make the extra effort and meet the parents in person if possible. This will give you an idea about what the puppy is accustomed to, how it was bred and what it is subconsciously aspiring to become.

The early breeding grounds define what the litter grows up into. Meeting the parents can therefore tell you a lot about what you are interested to know!

3) The Questions to Ask Yourself

Caring for a dog (any dog for that matter) is not easy. It is a massive responsibility that you willing take on yourself. It not only consumes a significant portion of your finances, it also demands a lot of your time and affection. Bringing a dog home is like having another family member!

Most people head into the relationship with their pets without much forethought. Such relationships, if not managed properly, usually end up in a mess. So if you are buying a Hungarian Vizsla just because "you have to have it", you are most probably headed in for trouble.

Here are a few questions that you should ask yourself before you get into the obligation. These questions will help you understand whether the companionship of the Hungarian Vizsla is precisely the thing that you need.

Keep in mind that there is no right or wrong answers; it all depends on you. But if, after going through the question answer session, you end up feeling a little confused about your decision, you should definitely give it more time to understand what you truly need.

1. Do I have the time and patience to endure what the puppy brings my way during its life?
2. As a puppy, it is challenging to help it blend in with you. As it grows into an adult, its needs change. While caring for a dog, there is a lot that you need to overlook in order to maintain a peaceful relationship. Do you really have it in you to allow your pet to grow old on you?
3. Is my lifestyle athletic, mediocre or towards the lazy end?

4. The general rule of thumb says most dogs are energetic – at least to some degree. So if you are one of the laid back types, you are probably more suited for a cat companion than a dog. You need to have some activity in your life to assure yourself (and the breeder) that you are up for the challenges put forth by your newfound pet.
5. How often do I have to travel?
6. Naturally, if you are travelling a lot, carrying a dog around with you can prove to be a nuisance. This does not mean doing so is impossible. It merely intends to imply doing so will be difficult for you! But if you can manage your travel plans with your dog, there shouldn't really be a reason to hold you back from it!
7. Can I tolerate the mess created by a dog?
8. For the first few days and weeks, you can rightfully anticipate a lot of mess created by your canine companion. This includes property damages as well as other accidents. Can you tolerate it and overlook these mistakes or are you the kind of clean freak that can't bear to see a smear on the mirror?! If you are one of the latter, petting a dog is probably the worst decision you can make. The plus point, however, with the Hungarian Vizsla is that it doesn't shed hair. Can't say the same about its habits though!
9. Do I have a family that demands my time and attention as much as the puppy would?
10. If you have a family, they would naturally want to be around you when you are home. If you can't manage a balance between your pet and your family, it is probably in your best interests not to acquire an additional responsibility. This applies particularly to those people who can put the dog out in order to care for their families – if you can't care for one, don't get one!
11. Am I physically fit enough to be caring for an active dog?
12. Caring for a dog is strenuous activity in itself. You might have to chase your pet all across the home, discipline it wherever required, clean up the mess along the way and also groom your pet time and again. With so much to do, a certain

level of physical fitness is recommended for you in order to make the companionship successful for both parties.

13. Can I afford my pet's expenses in whatever I earn?
14. The companionship of a canine doesn't come cheap. It has its own set of expenses. Keep in mind that as the puppy grows older, its expenses will most probably increase. You need to be prepared for this kind of expenditure beforehand. For a realistic estimate, read through the section on upkeep expenses carefully.
15. Exactly who is bringing in the dog; is it the children or me?
16. Children don't generally understand the complete picture when they insist on a pet dog. For the most part, they would lose interest readily. So if you are bringing in the pet solely on children's insistence, you need to have a backup plan – who will take care of the dog once the children are through with their craze? But if you are prepared to take the responsibility of the dog regardless of what the children do later on, it makes sense to go through all the trouble of getting the perfect dog for your family.
17. Do I know everything that I need to know about the specific dog breed I am planning to purchase?
18. Knowing about the dog breed helps you evaluate whether it would be able to adjust with your lifestyle and your family or not. It also keeps you on guard against fraudulent breeders. So research as much as you can about the dog breed before you head out of the door to get one; it is for your own good!
19. Why do I need a dog in my life?
20. Probably you are not really looking for a dog companion. It is possible that your canine companion is a way to vent out anger or loneliness. If you are actually looking for a life partner, it is best if you look through the right channels to get there. And if you are looking for something to kill time, pick a hobby. The Hungarian Vizsla (or any other dog for that matter) is an entity on its own. If it is not the thing you are really looking for, it is best you stay away from such experiments that are destined to go wrong.

When and if you have satisfactory answers to these questions, and you understand truly what you are headed into, only then you should decide to move forward with your purchase. As an educated and knowledgeable person, you are expected to exhibit some civic sense. Be a responsible person; make your decisions wisely. And once you've made them, stand by them to the end!

4) The Questions to Ask the Breeder

So you think you are ready to take on the responsibility of adopting a Hungarian Vizsla? If you've really decided, and you believe it is a right decision on your behalf, the next step is to head out and look for an authentic breeder.

Some of the things that you need to look out for have already been mentioned previously. For instance, make sure you ask for the registration papers and the medical certificates of the parents. Also, try to meet the parents in person if there is a possibility.

Take your time to establish whether the breeder you've selected is actually the one you are looking out for; if you have this part of the equation completed correctly, there are fewer chances your experiment will go wrong at a later stage.

Besides this, approach the dog clubs in your region for guidance. They will be able to get you in touch with those breeders that they deem reliable. This is a sure way to stay away from trouble.

If you are through with these stages and you are still looking for ways to figure out whether the breeder is genuine or not, here are a few questions you can ask to put your concerns at ease.

1. How long have you been involved with the Hungarian Vizsla breed? How many litters have you witnessed?
2. What particular aspects of the breed do you like?
3. How frequently is the litter expected? Do you use the same set of parents for each litter?
4. How are the parents of the litter? Are they present on site?

5. How and where are the littermates kept?
6. Are there any genetic problems associated with this breed?
7. Were the parents certified before they were allowed to mate?
8. Are you a member of any kennel club?
9. Are the medical records of the puppy available for scrutiny?
10. What are the terms and conditions stated in the contract?
11. What does the guarantee cover include?
12. Are there any references available with respect to previous customers?
13. Has the puppy or its parents been a part of any dog events?
14. Do you breed a particular dog breed or have you had experience breeding several different ones?
15. When was (or would be) the litter separated from its siblings and parents?
16. When will the puppy be ready to go to its new home?
17. How are the puppies being socialized?
18. Is the selected puppy or any of its siblings reported ill with serious medical conditions?
19. How many visits to the veterinary doctor have been made?
20. What is the puppy being fed currently?
21. What does caring for the Hungarian Vizsla imply?
22. How can the dog be best trained and disciplined?
23. How often does the Hungarian Vizsla need to be groomed?
24. What is the typical size of an adult Hungarian Vizsla?
25. Is it a social dog breed or will it make adoption of other pets difficult?
26. For how long can the Hungarian Vizsla survive on its own?
27. Does it need to be micro chipped or tattooed?

The genuine breeder will be able to put all your concerns at ease. If you are not getting any satisfactory answers from the breeder, it is a sure sign of trouble. This is one reason why you are encouraged to conduct a detailed research about the dog breed you intend to purchase.

Asking questions is your right! If the breeder shows signs of agitation, it is most probably because s/he does not have the kind of answers required to satisfy concerns. You are encouraged to ask as many questions from the breeder as you like.

A genuine breeder will look upon these questions as genuine care and interest; the unprofessional breeder will look upon these questions with contempt. Know the difference between the two!

When you are fully satisfied with the breeder, then you can begin worrying about picking the right puppy from the litter. But before that, it is possible for the breeder to want to know about your life as well.

The question answer session is primarily a two-way communication channel. The next section talks about the questions you can expect the breeder to ask from you. Be prepared with the right answers to make the transition honest and easy.

5) The Questions to Expect From the Breeder

A genuine breeder will be interested to know about you, your habitat and your lifestyle. It is important for the puppy to have the same or similar personality to yours in order to blend in well. If there is a high contrast between your pet's needs and your lifestyle, conflicts will arise inevitably.

Here are some of the questions you can expect the breeder to ask from you. Keep in mind that at this point, the breeder has both yours and your pet's best interests at heart. So if you plan to phrase answers that are not true, you will be inviting trouble at a later stage.

Just to give you an idea, here's what you can expect the breeder to ask from you.

1. How do you regard your lifestyle? Will you consider it to be laid back, athletic or somewhere in the middle?

2. Did you have any experience dealing with dogs and puppies before now?
3. Do you live with other pets or any small children? A new puppy can be expected to rebel and try to harm other living beings. So if there are kids involved, it is best to keep them away from interaction till the time your puppy has settled.
4. Where do you live? Some dog breeds are not suitable for apartment life. The Hungarian Vizsla, for the most part, will be able to adjust to all kinds of accommodations as long as it is not kept outdoors.
5. What is the purpose of adoption? Is it a short-lived fad or a long-term association that you are willingly and knowingly walking into? The breeder wants to know whether the future of the little puppy will be secure with you or not.
6. Have you researched about the breed? For the most part, the breeder will want to hear a response in the affirmative. But if you haven't really researched well, it is best if you say so outright. The breeder might cross question you to verify your claim – it will surely give-away your position on the case.
7. Are you aware of the costs associated with the upkeep of your pet?

The basic purpose of this interrogation is to understand how well-prepared you are to take up the responsibilities of a pet. During this interrogation, you might be able to make some observations yourself that will help you better register with what you really want.

One advice; be absolutely honest with the breeder. S/he might help you make a wiser choice when it comes to dog breeds. Similarly, it will also save you from a relationship that is destined to fail.

6) Selecting the Right Puppy From the Litter

Just like every person is different from another, every pet is unique. You cannot expect siblings to act alike even though they are related by blood. Same goes for the littermates as well.

The idea is to select the right puppy from the litter. The breeder will do his/her best to match the puppy rightly with the family.

However, selecting the puppy isn't that easy. Some people like to go for the physical appearances while making the selection. Some might be able to make an instant connection with a specific puppy and will therefore plan to take it home. The key is to make smart choices from the beginning to build a favorable association later on.

Here are some of the pointers which will help you steer away from puppies that have the tendency to develop behavioral issues. Remember, you are looking at a long term association, not an opportunity to show off a badly behaved pet before it is put out of the house!

1. It is good to have playful and active puppies. But is there a particular puppy that tries to dominate others? For instance, during a tug of war, is there a particular puppy that likes being on top at all times? This one is likely to have a highly dominating personality. Consequently, it will be quite some challenge to discipline this one. You want a puppy that is well-balanced and has the kind of sportsman spirit that wins everyone's hearts!
2. Dogs like playing with toys. But do they like sharing these too? If there is a puppy that doesn't allow others to play with its toys, it points towards an imminent behavioral problem. You are looking for a puppy that plays with its toys, allows others to play with these and will be more than willing to play with other littermates' toys as well.
3. In most cases, littermates are the first friends that the puppies make and will therefore move in groups at all times. If there is a loner somewhere who likes staying away from the pack, it is a sign of behavioral problems in future. A social puppy makes a good companion as it adjusts well with the family.
4. For puppies, one of the most natural games is the tug of war. It is often accompanied with biting. Usually, puppies understand when to let go – when they are actually hurting the

other party. But if there is a particular dog that fails to understand this, it points towards behavioral issues. At the later stage, this one is likely not to understand when its playful biting will become a major pain for the owner.

5. If a puppy is social, you have a major part of the problem resolved. If a puppy is particularly adverse to humans, it will rebel the ownership with all its might. Therefore it is in your best interests to look for a puppy that blends in well with pcople. At a later stage, this will help prevent unintentional accidents as well.

Puppies with behavioral problems can become quite a handful. The same stands true for rescue dogs as well. While it is a good gesture if you want to help a rescue dog by adopting it, it is best left to those who have prior experience handling dogs. If you are new to this ownership, don't get carried away. Learn about the art of dog keeping by adopting a puppy; you can later opt to help rescue dogs!

All dog enthusiasts and experts agree unanimously on one thing; breeding is the most crucial part of the adoption cycle. If the puppy is bred rightly, it will be less prone to all sorts of problems. However, if this isn't the case, then you are most surely entering into an unwise deal.

If you have secured your concerns on this end, it will definitely help you a lot in building a truly memorable relationship with your pet. It's all in the genetic code!

Chapter 4: Physical Characteristics

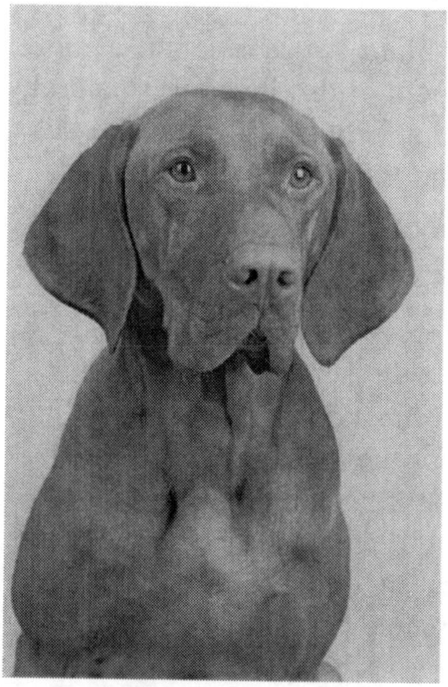

The Hungarian Vizsla is one of a kind. It is unique and possesses certain distinct characteristics which help in differentiating this breed from the rest. Here are some of the most profound physical characteristics that give the Hungarian Vizsla its identity.

Keep in mind that there are a few breeds that are quite similar in some regards. For instance, it is common for people to confuse between the Hungarian Vizsla and the Weimaraner dog breed. These breeds share quite a few physical characteristics. However, there are a few areas where notable differences can be observed.

To find out more about how the Vizsla looks and acts, read through this chapter carefully. This will not only help you in identifying this breed but will also help you distinguish it from the rest. This information can prevent you from getting in trouble with the breeder.

As you read about this wonderful breed, you will surely fall in love with it!

1) Their Origin

As mentioned previously, the Hungarian Vizsla originated from the country of Hungary. The gene pool of this breed was naturally cross bred with a number of other dog breeds that came into this region as a result of subsequent conquests. Although the Vizsla has retained most of its original characteristics, it has adapted a great many from other dog breeds.

During the World War II when Hungary was seized from its rulers, attempts were made to eliminate this breed. At the time, this dog breed signified royalty. Elimination of this breed signified the fall of the kingdom. For the most part, this propaganda was quite successful in the region of Hungary. However, during the migrations out of the country, a few Hungarian Vizslas also found their way out. This is how the breed survived the deliberate attempt to put an end to this breed.

The Hungarian Vizsla was initially a hunting dog used to hunt down certain unique birds. However, with time, as people became concerned about environmental conservation, this activity was stopped. This is where the Hungarian Vizsla came to be taken in for companion dogs.

It is believed that the Hungarian Vizsla has received its coat color from Turkish quail-hunting dogs and its pointer capabilities from western breeds. Apart from this, the Hungarian Vizsla is also believed to have been cross bred with hound dogs. This has fashioned the personality of this dog breed.

2) Salient Physical Features

The Hungarian Vizsla is a medium sized dog known for its hunting and pointing properties. It has a lean structure that aids in its rapid movement. This aspect of the dog is perfectly aligned with its hunting capabilities.

Apart from this, the Hungarian Vizsla does not have hair. It does not have the undercoat that is typical for most other dog breeds. For this reason, it is strongly recommended never to leave the Hungarian Vizsla stranded outdoors.

The Hungarian Vizsla is naturally a cleaner dog. It doesn't shed – majorly because it doesn't have the kind of hair it needs in order to shed it. Besides this, the Hungarian Vizsla is known to lick itself clean from time to time.

The absence of the undercoat and the fact that the Hungarian Vizsla likes to keep itself clean contributes towards another unparalleled aspect of the dog – it is relatively an odor-free breed. There is no typical "dog" smell about the dog. It may develop what some people recognize as a weak "wet dog" smell after taking a bath in pools or lakes but a shower at home will usually suffice to eliminate this odor.

The Hungarian Vizsla as a whole seems to have a seamless coat. This is because its body, nose, nails, eyes and paws are generally for more or less the same color. The rusty gold color may have gradients but it doesn't differ much. This gives the Hungarian Vizsla a solid color.

The Hungarian Vizsla has a lean body that helps with its hunting behaviors. The leanness adds to its pace and strength.

Most importantly, the Hungarian Vizsla has pointing capabilities. In the previous days when this breed was used for hunting rare bird species, the Hungarian Vizsla would point out the presence of a bird in the vicinity by going absolutely rigid in the body. Its nose would be pointing the way towards the bait. This served as a silent symbol of hunting prey in the perimeter. The Hungarian Vizsla still retains its hunting features though since the dog is no longer used for hunting pleasures, it does not exhibit such properties often.

Besides this, the Hungarian Vizsla is known to be a retriever as well. It does not only point out the presence of a bird but also retrieves the prey once it has been hunted down. More so, it retrieves without doing any damage to the hunted bird. These characteristics, coupled with its pointing capabilities, earned the Hungarian Vizsla the title of a gun dog – those dogs that specialize in hunting activities.

3) Coat Colors

For the Hungarian Vizsla, a rusty golden colored coat is a must. This breed usually does not have a lot of hair. This means its skin color becomes more prominent.

If anything, the coat can also be defined as copper colored, dark sandy golden or russet gold. However, a deeper mahogany color or a light sandy colored coat is considered as a disqualification.

Small white colored patches on the dog's neck, tail and fore-chest are permissible although they are not really preferred according to the breed standards given by renowned dog clubs around the world.

Some Vizsla variations will also have a saddle-type pattern across the back. Besides this, any variation in the coat color makes the specimen eligible for disqualification.

Besides this, another important identifier about the Hungarian Vizsla is that its nose will always be of a reddish brown color that blends in well with its coat. If this part is of any other color, it is a sign that the dog belongs to some other breed. For the Hungarian Vizsla, a reddish brown coat and nose is the surest form of identification.

4) Height and Weight

A mature male Hungarian Vizsla has a height of 22 inches to 25 inches (54 cm to 66 cm) and weighs between 45 lbs to 66 lbs (20 kg to 30 kg). In contrast with this, the female Hungarian Vizsla is slightly smaller.

A mature female Hungarian Vizsla has a height of about 21 inches to 24 inches (52 cm to 60 cm) and weighs between 40 lbs and 55 lbs (18 kg to 25 kg).

This adequately explains why the Hungarian Vizsla is considered to be a medium sized dog.

5) Life Expectancy

The Hungarian Vizsla can typically live up to 15 years.

However, the problem with the Hungarian Vizsla is that this breed is prone to a wide range of hereditary problems. This implies that there is a high probability for your Hungarian Vizsla to fall ill pertaining to health complications. Consequently, its life may be cut short.

Nevertheless, with the right kind of care and medical help, you can cherish up to 15 years of memories with your Hungarian Vizsla pet.

6) Litter Size

Typically, the litter size for a Hungarian Vizsla is 6 to 7 puppies. However, both larger litter size and smaller litter size have been recorded. The Hungarian Vizsla can give birth to about 12 puppies in one litter! Admittedly, this is a rare case.

7) Personality

The Hungarian Vizsla is labeled Velcro for a reason. It is because the breed is exceptionally friendly with people – especially the owners – that the breed won this name. The Hungarian Vizsla is inseparable from its owners. It clings to its human masters like no other dog breed. So you need to be prepared for this kind of responsibility before you head off to buy a Hungarian Vizsla.

The Hungarian Vizsla, in general, owns a pleasant and gentle personality. It can be trained and disciplined quite easily. It is "demonstrably" amiable and sensitive. Most people do not face a lot of problems trying to tame this breed. They make outclass companions and are quite popular for these traits.

The Hungarian Vizsla can distinguish between friends and foes quite effectively. For instance, if a person is apparently invading the Hungarian Vizsla's space, it will firstly try to limit this intrusion by barking profoundly. Although biting cases have not been reported as such, the Hungarian Vizsla may do so if it feels threatened that way.

The Hungarian Vizsla dogs are quite energetic and will need the owners to have an active lifestyle. This implies a weekly hiking or jogging trip or a daily walk at least. The Hungarian Vizsla can get fidgety if they are not exercised adequately.

The best part about the Hungarian Vizsla which comes as a part of their Velcro personality is that they are extremely loyal. They like staying by their owners' side at all times. They like exercising alongside the owner and will go all lengths to demonstrate their affection. The Hungarian Vizsla rarely goes savage.

The Vizslas prefer having a "job" to do – even if it is utterly effortless - they like being of service. A Hungarian Vizsla that is not responsible for any chore can become quite challenging to handle.

8) Intelligence

The Hungarian Vizsla is an intelligent breed. You can figure that out by their "pointing" capabilities. They have the tendency to tip off the bait by going rigid in the body and pointing their nose in the desired direction. This is the reason they were earlier used for hunting activities.

Another important indicator of the fact that the Hungarian Vizsla is an intelligent breed is that they are easily trainable. There are only a very few from this breed that possess extremely stubborn personalities. For the most part, Hungarian Vizsla are not a dominating breed. But if they are not being exercised properly, they might be prompted to test their limits. This might translate into property damage and other similar costs.

The Hungarian Vizsla is said to have a mind of its own. If an interesting sight catches its attention, it may ignore your calls or gestures. It'd be too engrossed in its activities to lend you an ear. This may become slightly irritating at times but for the most part, this behavior can be countered by effective training and counseling.

The Hungarian Vizsla dogs are also labeled as self-learners. They can learn basic actions and their meanings relatively easily. This poses a major contrast between the Hungarian Vizsla and other pointer breeds.

On the whole, the Hungarian Vizsla is quite intelligent. It takes some patience to let the Vizsla "grow" on you but once it has, it will be the beginning of a truly wonderful journey up ahead.

9) Preferred Living Conditions

The Hungarian Vizsla is a medium sized dog. It can therefore adjust in most homes with ease – it doesn't occupy a lot of space. But when it comes to its activity levels, it is best to have at least a small yard or a similar space where it can exercise easily.

Experts agree that the Hungarian Vizsla is not recommended for apartment life – not until and unless you are a daily walker and you can take it out regularly to exhaust its energy reserves.

The Hungarian Vizsla needs to exhaust its energy reserves in order to remain tame and amiable. If it does not receive regular exercise, it will readily become savage. The yard makes sure its destructive instincts do not materialize indoors!

Apart from this, the Hungarian Vizsla is quite fitting for hikes and exploratory trips around different landscapes. The companionship of a Hungarian Vizsla is quite rewarding in a number of ways – if you know how to counter the downsides. Easy trainability calls for added advantages.

10) Other Vital Statistics

Here are a few other vital statistics you can expect to observe about your Hungarian Vizsla. This will help you recognize whether your Hungarian Vizsla is healthy or not.

1. Temperature: 100.5 to 102.5 degrees Fahrenheit (38.05 to 39.16 Celsius).
2. Respiratory Rate: 10 to 20 per minute.
3. Pulse: Puppies, 120 to 160 per minute. Adults, 60 to 140 per minute.
4. Gums: should be pink.
5. Eyes: should be clear and lively. No unexplained discharges to be tolerated.

Chapter 5: Temperament

Those were some of the apparent characteristics you can expect to see in a Hungarian Vizsla. What it is really like to live with a Hungarian Vizsla; keep reading to find out!

One thing is for sure; the Hungarian Vizsla offers an extremely unique experience for you. You will surely remember it for the rest of your life as a "companion like no other"!

Here are some of its temperamental characteristics you should be aware of before you head off into a relationship with it.

1) Is it a Workaholic?

The Hungarian Vizsla is relatively less of a workaholic than its counterparts. The Weimaraner for instance is a lot more energetic than the Vizsla and will therefore pose a significant amount of challenges in disciplining the breed.

With the Hungarian Vizsla, the key is to exercise it daily. If its energy reserves are not being exhausted, they have the tendency to become destructive. A daily walk is therefore essential. Alternatively, if you assign it a particular task, it will be sufficient to keep it busy.

The activity does not necessarily have to be physical exhaustive – even if they are simply sitting and watching you perform your daily chores, it would be enough to keep them from clawing or chewing your sofas and other similar furniture pieces around the house!

Keep in mind that the Hungarian Vizsla is not suitable for outdoor environments. This is because the breed is short haired and does not have an undercoat. This means it cannot adjust with changing temperatures. So if you are planning to put it on guarding duties, it will most probably not work out well for both parties!

The Hungarian Vizsla is to be taken in as a companion dog instead of a guarding dog. Keep this in mind while building the relationship.

2) Behavior around Children

As mentioned previously, the Hungarian Vizslas are Velcro dogs. This implies that the breed is good with people. Therefore, it would not be much of a problem to get the Hungarian Vizsla to adjust with children.

However, it is strongly recommended not to leave the Hungarian Vizsla or the children without supervision – not unless the dog has been trained and the two parties have accepted each other's presence in the house.

With small children, it gets a little more challenging as the young ones do not understand what can put off the Hungarian Vizsla. At the same time, the Hungarian Vizsla does not understand what can or cannot hurt the little one. You'll need to train both parties to reciprocate each other's emotions.

It takes a little time for the children as well as the Hungarian Vizsla to get used to each other; if you can get through this time peacefully, it will help you build an inseparable relationship between the two.

3) Behavior around Other Pets

As Velcro dogs, the Hungarian Vizsla is naturally addicted to its owners. This means it will not be very willing to share its time with other pets. It will take a lot of disciplining and training to get the Hungarian Vizsla to recognize the presence of another pet in the house.

It is natural for the pets to compete with each other in order to gain the owner's attention. For the association to work well for all involved parties, it is important for you to train all pets to socialize with each other. Once they get used to it, they will be able to survive well alongside each other!

4) Is It An Escape Artist?

This is a tricky question. The breed itself cannot really be labeled generically as an escape artist. It largely depends on the kind of conditions that dog is being kept in.

Its Velcro nature has a lot to do in defining whether it tries to escape or not. On the whole, the Hungarian Vizslas are pretty obedient and affectionate - they like being around their owner all the time. Even if they are given meager roles like carrying a backpack or fetching something, they'd be happy just to be around the owner.

But if their need for human contact is not being met, it can become a little challenging to handle. This is when the Hungarian Vizsla will try to escape captivity through all possible means. It will damage property and try to find a way out into the open. It can turn the slightest possibility into a major escapade.

Once it breaks free, the Hungarian Vizsla will be hard to find. A Hungarian Vizsla that runs away is almost as though it is gone for good. Keeping it locked up in confined regions is therefore not a good idea.

This is the main reason why it is advised to exercise the Hungarian Vizsla if you are planning to leave it alone for some time. It cannot tolerate loneliness. A Hungarian Vizsla that is left on its own without exercise can bring down the entire house!

On a similar note, if you try to keep the Hungarian Vizsla confined to an area and try to discipline its rebellion through punishments, it will most likely lead to neurotic and behavioral problems. The Hungarian Vizsla will no longer be easy to tame. More so, it may even try to harm you in order to escape from the confinements.

If cared for in the right manner, the Hungarian Vizsla is not an escape artist. But if you are unable to provide for its "people" needs, it will try to escape in every possible way. This is why it is important to treat the Hungarian Vizsla in the right manner in order to retain its companionship!

The Hungarian Vizsla is one of a kind. It is amiable and works well with other beings. Even so, it has certain specific needs which, if not fulfilled, can compel the dog to make the run. It is therefore important for you to be aware of your pet's needs – this is what keeps it faithful to you!

Chapter 6: Evaluating the Pros and Cons

The Hungarian Vizsla is an amazing breed. You'll find a million reasons to choose the Hungarian Vizsla as your pet. But you need to be careful to evaluate the positives and the negatives equitably.

With the Hungarian Vizsla, it is not all fun and games. There are a few grey areas that you need to be prepared to tackle. Here the good and bad about the Hungarian Vizsla. If after going through this chapter you still feel you want to pet a Hungarian Vizsla, then go for it! It is most probably because this is what's best for you!

1) The Good Part about Hungarian Vizsla Ownership

There are quite a few positives attached with petting a Hungarian Vizsla. Here's why you would be inclined to pet this breed.

1. The Hungarian Vizsla is short haired. This means the breed does not shed hair. This calls for lesser mess around the house and fewer grooming concerns. So if you are particularly worried about picking up dog hair from uncanny places, this breed will solve it. This however does pose a challenge of its own.
2. The Hungarian Vizsla is sociable. This means it blends in well with people. So there will be fewer adjustment problems when you bring in the pet for the first time. It is generally good with people as well as with other animals.
3. It is easily trainable. It is an intelligent breed that can self-learn a number of tasks and responsibilities. It is particularly popular for its trainability. So you will fewer problems trying to teach important values to your pet!
4. It is a medium sized dog. This translates into higher manageability. Large dogs occupy a lot of space in the house and can be difficult to accommodate. On the other hand, small dogs have the tendency to hide in small places and be lost to sight. The Hungarian Vizsla falls in the middle of spectrum

and will therefore be appropriate for most of your petting needs.

5. The Hungarian Vizsla is an energetic and lively breed. It requires adequate exercise on daily basis to keep it from destroying your property. This in turn encourages you to follow an active lifestyle! It may actually help you transform your life around healthy living principles.

2) The Concerns over Hungarian Vizsla Ownership

Here are some of the downsides of petting a Hungarian Vizsla. You need to be prepared to tackle these challenges in order to build a sound foundation of companionship.

1. The Hungarian Vizsla is not an outdoor pet. It does not have an undercoat or hair on its body. This is one reason why it cannot be left out alone at night or during the winter season. It has to be kept indoors.
   In fact, you might be required to invest in a heating system to give it the ideal living conditions. If it is left out during a cool night or is not providing the ideal environment for any reason, it will readily fall ill.
   This is one reason why the Hungarian Vizsla is not suitable for the role of a guardian dog. If you are planning to purchase this breed for this purpose, you'll face serious disappointment in this regard.
2. The Hungarian Vizsla is prone to a number of health problems. Most of these are inherited. This means if you are not careful about selecting the breeder, you might have to give up on the association before time.
   Even so, the Hungarian Vizsla will need regular visits to the veterinary doctor in order to identify the problem when it is beginning to happen. Most of the medical conditions are inevitable. It will be extremely painful to let go of your companion in such a manner.
3. The Hungarian Vizsla needs substantial amount of space to live. It does not work well in confinements. So if you live in an apartment or do not have access to a backyard for any

reason, it might be best if you don't purchase a Hungarian Vizsla. It will either develop certain behavioral problems or damage your property in retaliation to your disciplinary activities.

4. The Hungarian Vizsla gets distracted easily. This might mean it will become irresponsive under certain circumstances. If you don't have the kind of patience that is required to settle with a Hungarian Vizsla, it is best left to those who do!
5. The Hungarian Vizsla can easily get inflicted with the infamous "Separation Anxiety". They crave human contact more than other breeds and can go through separation anxiety even if you leave them on their own for a couple of hours. Some people refer to this behavior as "clingy" but that's the way it is with the Hungarian Vizsla. If you don't know how to tackle that, you might run into some serious problems with your pet.
6. The Hungarian Vizsla will take some time to get comfortable around other people and in the new home. At times, this time frame may be substantially larger than other breeds. This means you need to be around more often and have to be careful around it. But it usually ends up well for both parties.
7. The Hungarian Vizsla is quite expressive. This means it jumps around when excited, barks and yaps for fun and may be wholly disturbing when it gets hyper. Exercise usually gets the vent up energy out of its system but you still need to be prepared for this kind of behavior.
8. The Hungarian Vizslas may be pretty unpredictable. There are no generalized characteristics. Every Vizsla is unique and may exhibit unique personality traits. You'll need to improvise accordingly. This book talks about the "typical" Hungarian Vizsla; if you end up with a special one, you'll need to adjust accordingly.

Chapter 7: The Acquisition Process

Now that you've understood the positives and negatives about petting a Hungarian Vizsla, it is time to decide whether this is the breed you really want to settle for. And if it is, the next section will come in particularly handy for you.

It all started with the breeder. If you've shortlisted the best breeder around town, you'll eventually end up with a well-behaved Hungarian Vizsla. Otherwise, you might be forced to end the relationship before time. Considering that the Hungarian Vizsla breed is prone to health problems further amplifies the need for professional breeding.

Here are a few tips and guidelines that will help you go through the acquisition process with ease.

1) Where to Buy a Hungarian Vizsla in the US?

For best results, you need to head off to the best there is. The American Kennel Club is the oldest dog club in America that offers recognition and registration for a wide range of dog breeds. The Hungarian Vizsla is luckily one of them.

So, while purchasing a Hungarian Vizsla in the United States, all you need to do is ask for the AKC papers from the breeder. If the breed is actually pedigree (most breeders will claim it to be so in order to add value to their offering), the AKC papers will prove it. If not, it most certainly points towards a problem.

The American Kennel Club offers registrations for pure breed dogs only. It is not like other dog registration agencies that provide documents without looking at the dog. There is a strict procedure being followed at the AKC to ensure the dog is pure breed. Even the slightest deviation from "typical standards" can disqualify the dog from this breed.

The AKC is the only dog organization that demands for the complete lineage of the dog to be known. For instance, it will not offer registration for any dog at random if the breeder calls them in. They will have to have records of the dog's parents, of its aunts and uncles and also grandparents if possible. The procedure is long drawn and cumbersome – and only the fittest survives the test. This is the reason AKC papers have so much value when it comes to dog certifications.

Another important thing to note about the AKC is that they can connect you with authentic breeders as well. They have a special forum on their website that delivers the information of reputable breeders in different states. This information is available with respect to the breed you are looking for in order to make it easier for you to find your companion. This effectively eliminates any concerns you may have about the authenticity of a breed or a breeder!

Be wary of online breeders – it is a lot easier to conduct fraud in online businesses. Until and unless you have a very strong reference for a specific business, it is best you don't go surfing for your companion online. Better still, don't make any payments before you've seen the specimen for yourself – if you've read through the previous sections carefully, you will definitely figure out a Hungarian Vizsla from other breeds.

Never settle for phone calls when it comes to breeders' references. It might be cumbersome to make the trip to a distant region but it usually pays off well in the end. Conducting fraud in phone calls is also quite possible. Don't believe anything till you've seen it with your own eyes and heard it for yourself!

Last but not the least; don't get the puppy shipped over to you. Instead, go over to the breeders and bring it to its new home. In doing so, you'll come to understand how the puppy was brought up, what it is accustomed to and how well it can settle down to the new environment. As said before, see for yourself before you make the final decision.

As far as the costs are concerned, we'll go through these in a little while. Keep reading to find out everything you need to know about the Hungarian Vizsla in order to build a long lasting and amiable relationship.

2) Where to Buy a Hungarian Vizsla in the UK?

The American Kennel Club operates in the United States and is considered as the primary evaluative measure there. In the United Kingdom, however, the AKC papers or registrations might not work as well.

In this part of the world, there is another important dog organization that is considered equivalent to the American Kennel Club. It is The Kennel Club.

Like the American Kennel Club, the Kennel Club also recognizes Hungarian Vizsla as a unique breed. It is categorized as a gun/sporting dog given its size and activity. The thing about the Kennel Club is this – it registers mixed breeds as well. So you will find complete information about the orientation of your puppy whether it is a pure breed or not.

Just like in the United States, you will come across several private breeders, puppy farms, professional breeders and pet shops where the Hungarian Vizsla can be purchased from. If you are hoping to play a role in the protection of dog gene pool and you want to discourage unethical breeding habits, you are advised to go for professional breeders only. Also, seek affiliation records of these breeders with renowned dog clubs such as the Kennel Club. This will further ensure the breeder follows recommended guidelines properly.

If you are going for online breeders, take time to figure out whether they are genuinely authentic breeders or not. Most authentic ones do not resort to online selling. If they are, then it pays to dedicate some extra time to decide whether it is fraud or not. When and if you've made a financial transaction in their favor, rest assured they won't be reversed as easily!

3) Estimated Prices for this Breed

Another important aspect of the acquisition process is the price you'll need to pay in order to purchase a Hungarian Vizsla dog. Keep in mind that the Hungarian Vizsla is an expensive breed. Since it is native to Hungary, you'll need to get it imported to your country. This adds up the cost of acquisition.

However, due to the rising popularity of this breed, it is possible for you to find local breeders that are involved in creating pedigrees for this breed. Here, the most important concern for you is to identify a genuine breeder!

In the United States, the initial cost of acquiring a Hungarian Vizsla ranges between $600 and $1200 depending on the age of the dog. An older dog is more likely to be trained and hence is likely to be more expensive. A rescue dog, on the other hand, is usually up for adoption without a price tag. But it is strictly not recommended for you to try taming a Hungarian Vizsla rescue dog without having any hands on experience with the breed!

The price cannot be considered as an indicator of the dog's quality or "pureness". For some professional breeders, it is more important for the dog to be taken in my responsible families than to make enough money. They may offer you the dog for extremely low prices if you exhibit the kind of enthusiasm and interest they are looking for!

In the United Kingdom, the Hungarian Vizsla is equally expensive if not more. In this part of the world, the prices start from £600 and can go up to several thousand depending on the age of the dog. For old dogs, a major part of the cost comes from its training. As in the US, rescue dogs are usually up for adoption without incurring any costs.

This is just the beginning. Keep in mind that the maintenance cost of the Hungarian Vizsla is equally high. This includes their edibles as well as other accessories that keep the dog occupied. While heading out to purchase the dog, it is a good idea to have a contingency plan for other recurring costs you will pay during the course of its lifetime!

4) Signs of a Healthy Hungarian Vizsla Dog

The association with pets is seldom built for shorter durations. When you are headed to purchase your Hungarian Vizsla, you should be prepared for over one decade of relationship with its fair share of troubles and memories.

This motive is eventually connected with the health of the Hungarian Vizsla dog. The healthier it is, the longer it will survive.

The quest for healthy pets should begin at the time you purchase it. If your Hungarian Vizsla dog faces any problems from day one, it is likely to aggravate through its lifetime.

While the veterinary doctor and the breeder (those who truly know about the breed) might be able to diagnose a problem beforehand, it is often not as easy for potential buyers like yourself to diagnose problems at such a stage. It is therefore advised for you to book an appointment with a reputed veterinary doctor well in advance so you can get your pet medically evaluated before taking it home.

Despite this, here are some of the factors you should keep in mind before purchasing your Hungarian Vizsla dog to ensure it is as healthy as possible!

a. Its Records

Ask the breeder to share your Hungarian Vizsla dog's heath records with you. This includes detailed information about its vaccinations and all other trips to the veterinary doctor that it might have made.

It wouldn't hurt to ask the breeder to get an "all-clear" certificate from a veterinary doctor on your behalf before you transfer the funds. This will further add towards the credibility of the breeder.

Though in case the breeder does provide you with any records, make sure you reach the veterinarian doctor to seek confirmation for the reports.

Much like every other breed, your Hungarian Vizsla will need to be vaccinated against a host of common dog diseases. However, it shouldn't happen very often.

The contemporary medicine is of the opinion that dogs don't need frequent vaccinations, that is, they don't need to be vaccinated every few weeks. At times, dogs might exhibit adverse reactions to frequent vaccinations. Make sure you are not taking any risks with your puppy.

On a similar note, beware of combination shots. Your breeder might suggest you give a 5-in-1 shot to your dog in order to save time. This can backfire.

It has been noted in several accounts that giving a Hungarian Vizsla multiple vaccinations in one go has created health complications for the puppy. If not identified in a timely manner, these vaccinations can seriously compromise the well being of the Hungarian Vizsla puppy. In any case, it is advised to seek a professional veterinary doctor's advice on how to draft up your puppy's schedule of vaccination.

At best, give it one vaccination at a time. If your puppy seems to be reacting badly to it, make a mental note never to repeat the same vaccinations over. Generally, vaccinations are injected more frequently during the early years than when the puppy is older. In case of the Hungarian Vizsla, the frequency needs to be tuned down further to make sure it doesn't impact your pet negatively.

Your Hungarian Vizsla will need to be vaccinated against parainfluenza, parovirus, leptospirosis, hepatitis, and distemper.

In the beginning, you would need to take your Hungarian Vizsla to the veterinary doctor every month, that is, the second, third and fourth month without fail. After the fourth month, the frequency of the shots will be reduced to once in a year.

Consult your veterinary doctor to find ways to ensure the vaccinations are well dealt with by the Hungarian Vizsla dog. In case any slightest disturbance occurs, rush to the veterinary doctor immediately to counter the adverse reactions. In the worst case scenarios, negligence may be accompanied by the death of the little one.

b. Some Physical Indicators

Before you get to the purchase stage, there are a few general signs of good health to be aware of when choosing a healthy puppy from a litter. These principles apply to all dog breeds equally. It includes:

1. **Breathing** – a healthy puppy will breathe quietly, without coughing or sneezing, and there will be no crusting or discharge around their nostrils.
2. **Body** – they will look round and well fed, with an obvious layer of fat over their rib cage.
3. **Coat** – a healthy puppy will have a soft coat with no dandruff, dullness, greasiness or bald spots. In the case of a Hungarian Vizsla, the coat will be extremely short and almost invisible. So you can feel its skin for unusual spots.
4. **Energy** – a well rested puppy will be alert and energetic. If it is the other way around, it is most probably a symbol of problem.

5. **Hearing** – a healthy puppy with good hearing should react if you clap your hands behind their head.
6. **Genitals** – a healthy puppy will not have any sort of discharge visible in or around their genital or anal regions.
7. **Mobility** – a healthy puppy will walk and run normally without wobbling, limping or seeming to be weak, stiff or sore. This comes in particularly handy while selecting the Hungarian Vizsla dog. The breed is prone to a wide range of musculoskeletal problems. So you need to be extra careful in evaluating its mobility.
8. **Vision** – a healthy puppy will have bright, clear eyes without crust or discharge and they should notice if a ball is rolled past them within their field of vision.

If your Hungarian Vizsla dog seems to be facing certain difficulty in any of these aspects, demand a veterinary inspection before signing the contract.

5) The Registration

Once you've purchased your Hungarian Vizsla dog, make sure you get it registered with the American Kennel Club if it is known to be a pedigree. This will ensure a generation of purebreds is adequately recognized if you chose to mate your pet.

Moreover, the AKC registration will also allow you to participate in a number of dog shows being held around the year in different parts of the world. This will help you get acquainted with other dog owners and to show off your amazing pet to masses.

If you are living in the United Kingdom, make sure you get your pet registered with the Kennel Club of UK. Since the Kennel Club registers both purebreds and mixed breeds, it will not be much of a problem for you to get your pet registered.

Play your role in eliminating unhealthy breeding practices. Get your pet registered so that it is eligible to be a part of numerous dog shows happening around the world.

Besides these important facts, which compel you to reconsider getting your Hungarian Vizsla dog registered with the relevant authorities, there are other benefits associated with the registration phase.

For instance, if your Hungarian Vizsla dog manages to escape from its bounds and ends up being captured by the authorities, its registration will keep it alive long enough to give you time to come and get it. If your pet isn't registered, it will be given comparatively smaller slice of time to be rescued. If there is no one to own the pet, it will subsequently be put to a never ending sleep. Registration, in effect, ensures longevity for your pet in a legal sense.

Getting your dog registered also saves you from unnecessary penalties. For instance, a registration or license may cost you about $10 to $20 at maximum. However, keeping your dog unregistered can cost you up to $200 in penalty. Decide for yourself – which cost would you rather pay?!

Registration also establishes your ownership over your pet. It is legally and emotionally yours. When it is a well accepted contract between you and your pet, why wouldn't you go just a step further to make sure the world recognizes it too? Dog registration can go a long way in determining how connected you are with your pet.

6) Decisions to Buy

There are several other important factors that you need to consider while purchasing the Hungarian Vizsla dog. Here are a few to get you started with streamlining your options and making the final purchase.

a. One, Two, or More?

How many Hungarian Vizsla dogs should you buy? Seeing their medium size and active nature, you might be inclined to purchase multiple dogs in one go. Who wouldn't want to be in a house full of medium sized, enthusiastic beings jumping all over the place? This is where you may be headed for serious trouble.

If you have no prior experience handling the Hungarian Vizsla breed, it is strictly recommended for you to pet one canine at a time. Despite their amiable natures, they may prove to be quite a handful once they are through with the initial adaptation phase. Who would've thought how troublesome they can get!

However, if you are absolutely positive about your decision to purchase multiple Hungarian Vizsla puppies in one go, feel free to go ahead. If you've socialized your pets adequately and you've transferred the right kind of values and discipline in your pets, it will be extremely rewarding to come home and be greeted by multiple pets at the door!

Beware of competition though. The Hungarian Vizsla dogs do not like being ignored. This is where purchasing multiple puppies in one go may prove to be more fruitful; if a new one is brought in after you've pampered the first one, it is bound to feel neglected and hence the number of problems and tantrums it is likely to throw will be higher. On the same note, make sure you are not over looking your resource availability – are you ready to take on the responsibility of more than one pet?!

On the other hand, if you are planning to pet different animals, make sure they complement each other. The Vizslas and the rodents or birds cannot survive together given the former's hunting instincts. They've a heritage of hunting these small animals! The Hungarian Vizsla may tolerate the presence of another dog or cat but not of other rodents or birds!

b. Male or a Female?

In the big picture, the gender of the Hungarian Vizsla does not matter. Both are equally affectionate and lovable. Both have roughly the same looks and size. Most of their physical and mental characteristics will match precisely. The only thing where it does matter is when you think about allowing your pet to raise its own family.

With the female dogs in general, the problems pertaining to "coming in heat" and "mating" may be quite painful for your canine friend as well as for you. Same is the case with the male Hungarian Vizsla though it is a little less daunting since the male ones do not have to face the repercussions of mating. It nevertheless is an issue that demands foresightedness and preplanning to make sure you have the contingency ready by the time the problem is thrust upon you!

Getting your pets spayed and neutered is one way of resolving this emotional conflict though it is quite debatable whether you should indulge in such an activity or not.

It most definitely alters the nature of your pet. It was born capable of procreation. Such an act can be considered as a serious violation of animal rights! It is a long winded debate whether one should or should not go for spaying and neutering. You will find more details about this topic in due time. Keep reading to find out all about it.

c. The Best Age?

The little ones receive their first nutrition from their mothers. Their first values are learnt from their littermates and from their mothers. It is therefore important to allow the Hungarian Vizsla dog enough time to receive the basic training from its mother before it is separated and put into different homes.

For the first two months, it is strictly recommended not to try separating the litter from its parents. The first eight weeks of its life are crucial in defining its progress through life. Puppies separated before this age might exhibit personality disorders at a later stage. They may also fall ill owing to the separation anxiety as at this tender age, they need their kind the most.

The Hungarian Vizsla puppies are usually up for adoption from the third or fourth week of its life. If you are planning to adopt these, make sure you put them through the right training courses at the right time to control behavioral problems from the beginning.

Once the puppies have stabilized, that is, after the first eight weeks of its life, you can try adapting it to the environment. This includes replacing the mother's nutrition with pet food, bringing the pet towards solid foods, incorporating the right amounts of liquids to its diet and so on and so forth. This is the ideal time for adoption!

Besides taking in puppies, you can also go for rescue dogs. They are the ones that come from battered homes and are themselves in a more or less battered state. You can provide shelter to these dogs till the time they meet their natural demise. Often, organizations working with rescue dogs do not charge anything to those caring for the dog.

This, however, translates into more troubles with the pet. They are more likely to have a host of health problems and may also have personality disorders which make taming them a little more difficult. So it is recommended to take in rescue dogs only if you have had prior experience dealing with exceptionally troublesome specimen of their kind!

Keep in mind that at both ages, the requirements of the Hungarian Vizsla will be very different. Make sure you are able to care for it in the way it deserves. It is the first stepping stone towards a healthy, long term relationship with your Hungarian Vizsla dog!

Chapter 8: Preparing to Bring Your Dog Home

So you are ready to bring the Hungarian Vizsla home? You've figured out the breeder you want to purchase the puppy from, you have a fair idea about how it is going to be and you are up for the challenge. It is the first stepping stone to mark the beginning of an awesome journey up ahead!

But before you actually bring your puppy home, you need to prepare for its arrival. Most breeders will hand over your pet in a (temporary) travel crate – it is the best they can do. The rest is up to you to decide!

Do you have a plan to accommodate your newfound pet yet? Where will it sleep? What will it eat? What kind of toys it will have? And other similar concerns that shape the first few weeks of your pet?

All of these questions need to be answered before you bring the pet home. By and large, you will not have the time or the energy to go out shopping within the first two weeks. You need to prepare in a way that keeps you home for a minimum of two weeks after you've acquired your pet!

Here are a few tips to prepare for your pet's entry in your life and home. Hope these will come in handy and prepare you for the toughest part of this association. Once the puppy has settled in, the going will get easier!

1) Puppy Proofing Your Home

There are quite a few alterations you will need to make to your house to make it fit for your Hungarian Vizsla dog. It is all in your best interests and for your pet's well-being.

Puppies, especially those that are teething, like nibbling at things they do not realize might be of importance to you – for instance, your sofa, your chairs, curtains and other accessories around the house.

They also like flexing their claws at things that are resistant like wooden doors.

Here is what you need to do to keep your property and puppy safe from damages.

1. A tall well-rooted fence around your home!

This is because Hungarian Vizsla dogs have an aptitude of digging in order to build its escape channel. Moreover, it will also try jumping over the fence in order to escape. So you need a tall fence in order to contain it within premises. Although it is not likely to do so all the time, it is best to have this contingency in place before your puppy tries to make the escape!

2. Install safety latches in every possible place.

This includes all cabinets and cupboards in the kitchen and elsewhere in the house that are used to stock toxic chemicals like cleaners etc.

You definitely don't want your Hungarian Vizsla dog to discover these or try experimenting with them.

Also, it is a good idea to install devices on the doors that enables them to close on their own. Keep nurseries, personal rooms and other similar places out of reach of your canine.

If your pet chokes on your child's toy or some other product of similar nature, rest assured the results are least likely to be pleasant!

Keep all medicines, chemicals, cleaners and other potentially hazardous solutions stored behind locked doors at all times!

3. Safe wirings

Under normal circumstances, leaving a wire or two lying haphazard on the ground is not a big problem; but this is not the case once you have a pet dog in the house.

Inquisitive as they are, they are likely to try playing with the unsheathed wire using their claws. During this little adventure, they might end up exposing the internal copper wirings which may lead to an electric shock.

It is therefore infinitely better to keep these wires stowed away from plain view in the corners of the room.

Also, use a protective covering made from durable plastic to prevent scratches.

Give your pet other safe objects to play with so the wires do not catch its attention!

4. Keep small, potentially dangerous and fragile items away from your pet's reach.

This includes all kinds of decoration pieces made from crystal, glass or other similar material that shatters on impact.

Also, all CDs, DVDs, keys, remotes, kitchen utensils, containers, sharp-edged items, plastic bags and other similar objects that have the tendency to become lethal should be stocked behind locked doors.

Your Hungarian Vizsla pet does not have as much sense to realize when it is headed for some major trouble. Care for it as you would if it were your offspring!

5. Pet door

You will need to install one in your main door to allow your dog to move in and out of the house as it pleases.

Make sure it is the right size and does not strangle the canine.

Also, make sure there are no obstructions to its course.

Alternatively, be prepared to see some claw marks on the door if your canine friend finds it closed when and if it needs to go outdoors. This also curtails the call of nature which might be quite messy to clean up.

Invest in a worthwhile pet door to make things easier.

6. Your washroom needs dog-proofing as well.

Keep the door closed at all times – use an automatic door lock if necessary.

The flush bowl is an exceptionally attractive place for your pet and it is equally hazardous too! And this does not even cover the dangers of slippery floors!

Best to keep the door of your washroom locked to ban your pet's entry into it.

If you are potty training your pet to use your washroom, make sure you never leave it there unattended until it has been trained properly.

7. Dog-foe plants, edibles and objects to be stored away from reach.

Surprisingly, most dogs don't tolerate chocolates well. So don't leave your wrappers lying around.

Also, if you have any plants that your pet is allergic to, you need to make arrangement to discourage contact. Either change the position of the plant or put it in a place where your pet is not allowed.

8. Use barriers where needed.

This applies equally to indoor uses as well as outdoor uses. You might want to proof your sofas and cabinets by using a barrier/grill.

Also, if you have an outdoor garden, don't ever leave your dog unattended until and unless you are looking for a major makeover!

Use barriers in front of pools and every other object you don't want your pet to sniff around. It is for its own good!

9. Be careful while using detergents, cleaners and other chemicals.

Their remains are still dangerous for your pet.

Also, garage should be free from chemicals if it is a "can-visit" area for your pet.

Keep your car in regular check to prevent leakages and spills.

Try your level best to keep your pet under supervision at all times. This way you get to control small and innocent mistakes from becoming life-threatening situations.

2) Inspecting the Extent of Puppy Proofing

Once you are satisfied with your proofing efforts, try looking at the situation from your puppy's point of view. Crouch down on all fours and look around your place from the eye level of a puppy. More often, you will not be able to look into the nook and corners from a higher vantage point as when you are standing upright.

Naturally, this means you might be overlooking a few crucial aspects of puppy proofing the house, which might emerge as a major threat later on!

You can turn this into a creative activity for the little ones in your house. Identify all possible hazards and threats and fix them as soon as possible. It is best if your puppy does not have the liberty to explore the hazards before you!

The first few days/weeks are extremely crucial for your pet to settle down. If you successfully make it through these tough days, rest assured there is a rainbow at the other end! It is always better to be safe than sorry. However, in case an accident has taken place or you suspect something is seriously wrong with your pet – probably because it has started acting very weird lately – don't waste a minute and rush it to a veterinary doctor!

A problem nipped in the bud is much better than a situation that needs to be controlled once it has already reached beyond your control! The rest should be fine!

3) Preliminary Shopping List for Your Hungarian Vizsla

Be fully prepared to receive your pet in a travel crate – it is the best that will be arranged by most breeders. As the pet is new and possibly bewildered, it is best not to carry it in your arms.

Besides this vital necessity (to make transportation possible), there are a dozen other things you will need to purchase so that your pet can survive a minimum of two weeks in the new home.

If you are planning to take your new pet for shopping even before it has settled, rest assured it is a sure recipe for disaster. Have enough stocks to last you two weeks before you bring the new one home. By this time, your pet will have adjusted to the new owner, new rules and new lifestyle. Hence it will pose fewer challenges while handling.

Here is a list of things you need to purchase – before the new one walks in!

1. Visit to the veterinary.

Call in to book your appointment if needed.

It is like a gift from you to your dog – something that it will definitely be thankful for even if it is not able to say it out loud.

Have it vaccinated for all major diseases and draft up a schedule for regular checkups. Mark it on your calendar so you don't miss out on it.

Remember, your vet can see beyond the short shiny coat and hence is in a better state to identify any imminent health problems and diseases.

As in the case of breeder, take your time in locating a certified and genuine veterinary doctor.

2. Pet Food!

This includes food, treats and all other form of edibles for your pet.

This is one thing you will need within 24 hours of getting the dog home. Moreover, this is one thing that is directly related to its health, rationality, irritability and resistance.

Try to get the same stocks of pet food your canine is already accustomed to at the breeder's – so it can feel at home. Be foresighted and get enough food to last you a minimum of two weeks.

3. Food and Water bowls.

As much as you would like it, your canine friends cannot feast with you using your kitchen utensils.

They need to have their own bowls for food and water. Make sure you have purchased these beforehand to minimize the stress of finding an alternative impromptu when the need arises.

Also, keep in mind that your pet associates these bowls with nutrition and will continue to do so for a long time. So it is a good idea to invest in high-quality and durable bowls.

Have a good look at the breeder's options before making your decision so that your new friend does not feel like a stranger.

4. ID tags, collars and leash.

These accessories mark your pet dog and establish your ownership for the world to see.

It is also imperative for you to get these affairs in order well before you get your new companion home. Feeling as a captive being taken away from home, your new pet is likely to make a dash into the unknown whenever it is given the opportunity.

Also, in a foreign neighborhood, chances of it finding its way to your home are next to impossible. So make sure your new friend is fastened adequately to your vehicle to prevent such unfortunate incidences.

Even if it does, the identification documents around its neck will prove to be a life savior – someone else who comes across your dog will be able to return it home if your dog carries its home address!

Keep the Hungarian Vizsla dog's size, strength and personality traits in mind while shopping for its identification accessories.

5. Dog bed.

After a long day of getting accustomed to foreign practices and obeying orders from a relatively unknown master, your dog needs adequate rest so that it wakes up fresh and healthy the next morning.

A dog bed lined with soft linens and soft cushions work well. If your pet does not sleep well, it will eventually lead it towards bigger health problems.

So make sure you place its bed in a secluded and silent corner of the house. Also, help your pet associate this space with "night" and "sleep" so it is easier to command it to rest.

Rest assured this is not something you can leave on for later – your canine friend needs a good night's sleep every night!

Since the Hungarian Vizsla dog does not grow too large, you might be able to use the same bed throughout its life. So invest wisely!

6. Dog toys.

Dogs don't sleep well with a whole lot of built up energy in their bodies. Assuming you don't have the time or the will to walk your pet every evening/morning in the first few days of association; dog toys are the second best alternative to achieve this motive.

It helps in keeping your pet occupied and entertained (without your active effort). Moreover, dog toys are also an effective way of stimulating the dog's brain and helping it develop its mental capacities.

Use intelligent dog toys and obstacles to help your canine friend develop intellectually and physically – as it would if it were to live in the wild!

7. Travel crate.

You won't need it immediately (unless your breeder fails to offer the initial carry crate) but you eventually will.

Imagine the first time you go out shopping after your new pet makes it home. How do you imagine you will carry the fragile being? Carrying it in your arms, though an impressive gesture, will not work well as your pet will feel threatened by the sudden presence of hundreds of other shoppers.

On top of this, there are other places you might need to go to – office, veterinary doctor, your own doctor and others – that will definitely not accommodate an "unfastened" dog. So it is better to purchase a travel crate well beforehand to keep away from embarrassments.

8. Dog Clothes.

This becomes exceptionally imperative if you are planning to purchase your Hungarian Vizsla companion during the winter.

Seeing that it doesn't have a lot of hair, you'll need to keep it covered at all times – especially during the winter months – regardless of whether it is indoors or not.

The cold can get to its skin and make it ill before you would realize what has happened.

Keep your defenses up to protect your pet against all odds.
If you can, invest in a room heater as well. If it gets too chilly, you'll need electric heaters to complement your dog's clothing.

9. Grooming Supplies

Dogs are inquisitive creatures. They have inexplicable interest in finding out what is hidden in the darkest of corners. They can easily be led to places by the smallest of insects. So naturally, they don't last a week without getting dirty.

With the Hungarian Vizsla, the absence of a hairy coat has its benefits but it also poses its own set of challenges. You will need to groom your Hungarian Vizsla on a weekly basis to keep it clean and presentable.

Having grooming supplies beforehand therefore is a good idea. Imagine having to go to the supermarket with an unkempt dog that clearly says its master does not care!

Be foresighted enough to prepare for things that are expected to happen. Make sure you search through all alternatives on the market before settling for a few – it helps you get the best possible items!
Also, make sure you have ample supplies to last two weeks. It would typically include a shampoo, scrub, dental hygiene solutions, nail clippers, hair tonic, conditioners, and everything else that you would like to use for your new pet's beauty! The sky is the limit!

Even so, it is recommended not to use a lot of chemicals on your pet as an excess of everything is detrimental!

10. Puppy Pads

No one likes to witness a trail of unsightly liquids or solids winded all across the house. The odor makes it even more unbearable. Do yourself a favor and use puppy pads for the first few days – especially if your canine friend is not yet potty trained. Train it to use the open outdoors for relieving itself. It will become possible and tolerable over-time!

Once you are out on the shopping spree, you will come across a number of other items that are not on this list but might apparently look useful. Evaluate its utility in the light of your pet's needs before making your purchase.

However, if it seems like an absolute necessity, it is better not to leave it for a later date.

Admittedly, these accessories summed up with the cost of acquiring a pet (payment to the breeder, registrations etc) can amount to a significant portion of your savings. So you need to be mentally prepared for this kind of expenditure.

It is expected to be an association of a decade or two; so rest assured it will be an ongoing expense rather than just a one-time incident!

Also, keep in mind that most of the items on your shopping list will last quite a few years before they become unusable, broken or "too small" for use (provided you make intelligent decisions in the first place!). So usually the returns on your investment are quite appreciable if you are looking long term.

Having a new companion inevitably calls for a few adjustments. You will need to make quite a few sacrifices to let your new friend settle in. But it will be worth the time and effort!

Chapter 9: The Initial Days

The first few days are always the trickiest. This is the time when your puppy feels threatened even by your presence. The puppy finds the “foreign” environment intimidating. It does not only miss its home but also its family. It is natural for the puppy to act a little weird – after all, it is trying to get accustomed to the new surroundings.

This is the time when you need to be patient with your puppy. If you try to get harsh with it, it might develop certain behavioral issues. This doesn’t imply you need to be extremely lenient with your newfound companion. Rather, you need to be firm and supportive.

This section covers in detail how you should tackle the first few days and weeks of your pet’s companionship.

1) The First Few Days and Weeks

Before bringing your new companion home, make sure you’ve put the right barriers in place. Sweep the floors carefully to eliminate all sources of discomfort for the puppy. Also, close the doors to your personal rooms. Your puppy does not need to have access to all rooms of the house. Just keep one or two doors open to the rooms that have been puppy-proofed.

Also, make sure you have at least two weeks’ puppy supplies readily available with you. Unless you have support at home, you won’t be leaving the premises for shopping before the second week. So it is best to have your act in order before the little one walks in.

For the first few weeks, you will have to let your Hungarian Vizsla get accustomed to the environment of your house. It will explore the territories and try to understand what is being expected of it in the given scenario.

It is important for you to be consistent with your puppy's routine – its sleep time, its feeding time, its exercise time, and so on and so forth. Inconsistency will give rise to personality disorders and irritability, which, in the long run, will impact you negatively!

The first few weeks are ideal for potty training; so invest in your efforts wisely. Let your puppy know where it can relieve itself and where it is considered inappropriate. Kennel training should also be conducted to establish your supremacy over your pet. The first few days and weeks are critical to the long-term relationship with your pet – make sure you are investing in its grooming wisely!

Also, never leave your puppy without supervision. If your puppy is allowed to have its way, it will most surely opt for disaster – for itself as well as for you. Keep a close eye on its activities and curb any evil intentions in the bud. This is important for a healthy relationship later on.

Last but not the least; stay strict but loving with your pet. It needs to know who the boss is but also needs to understand that it is being loved. Don't make it feel too neglected or troubled – it will try to make the run. If it is being pampered too much, it will begin considering itself as the "leader". Establish a balance so the relationship can be carried forth ideally!

2) Setting the Rules

First and foremost, before you begin training your pet, you need to lay out a few rules in a language that it understands. It may be rules like where to relieve, what to do for play, the rooms which are out of bounds for it, and others. You will also need to establish certain hand gestures or words associated with specific actions or meanings.

The first and foremost rule that you need to set is to establish your supremacy over your pet. It needs to understand that you are the only leader in the house. Even with the dominant nature of dogs, your pet needs to understand and register your control. It needs to be subservient to you. It needs to understand that it is in no position to challenge its master. And integration of this value begins when you bring the puppy home.

Never let your puppy lead you into the house. It should always be the one following you around. Make sure all human beings are entering the house before the puppy – it tells the dog where it stands in the hierarchy. With the Hungarian Vizsla, it may not be as easy.

As the Hungarian Vizsla is a Velcro dog, it becomes a little difficult to resist its sprightly behavior. Nevertheless, if you are looking for a well behaved puppy, you will need to harden yourself and treat it as you would treat a bigger dog. All dogs essentially have the same nature – they need to be treated alike in order to keep them disciplined.

Besides this, keep the no-puppy zones in your house locked at all times. If you see your puppy trying to break in, let it know this behavior is undesirable. Penalize it if necessary – it will not try to transgress limits once it understands.

Let your puppy know where it is supposed to sleep, eat, or drink. Also, build a schedule for its activities – when it is supposed to feast or sleep. Administer these values so the Hungarian Vizsla is less challenging when it matures.

3) Common Mistakes to Avoid

There are several mistakes you are most likely to commit while caring for your pet. You won't indulge in these mistakes deliberately – it rather happens unintentionally. Nevertheless, it can have long lasting impact on your puppy's grooming and discipline.

Here are few of the most common mistakes people are known to make with their pets:

1. **Let the puppy sleep in bed with you.** It is a sure recipe for disaster. You let the puppy believe it is equivalent – if not superior – to you.
2. **Free feeding.** That is another way of reinforcing its dominating characteristics. It should be made to follow a feeding schedule.
3. **Playing too hard or too long.** It will begin reflecting on the puppy's health. Let it rest adequately.
4. **Petting heavily because it's a Velcro dog.** For the first few days, you'll be inclined to give it more attention. Keep in mind that you are actually building expectations in your puppy's mind. Once it has become accustomed to your petting frequency, it will be difficult to change this habit.
5. **Grooming.** Get your pet accustomed to grooming procedures. If it becomes averse to frequent grooming, well then best of luck with the Hungarian Vizsla dog!
6. **Putting it outdoors.** The Hungarian Vizsla cannot survive in the outdoor environment. You will need to keep it indoors, especially during the winter months, if you want to keep it from falling ill.

4) Ways to Bond With Your Hungarian Vizsla

The Hungarian Vizsla is a sprightly dog with a lot of energy and love to share. You will begin bonding with your Hungarian Vizsla puppy from the very first moment you bring them home from the breeders.

This is the time when your puppy will be the most upset and nervous, as they will no longer have the guidance, warmth, and comfort of their mother or their other littermates, and you will need to take on the role of being your new puppy's center of attention.

Be patient, kind, and gentle with them as they are learning about you being their new center of the universe.

Your daily interaction with your puppy during play sessions and especially your discipline exercises – including going for walks on leash, and teaching commands and tricks – will all be wonderful bonding opportunities.

Do not make the mistake of thinking that *"bonding"* with your new puppy can only happen if you are playing or cuddling together, because the very best bonding happens when you are kindly teaching rules and boundaries, and this intelligent puppy will be most eager to learn.

What Does the Wag Mean?

It can be a mistake to automatically assume that if a dog is wagging their tail that they are happy and friendly.

When determining a dog's true intent or demeanor, you need to take into consideration the entire dog because it is entirely possible that a dog can be wagging its tail just before it decides to take an aggressive lunge toward you.

More important in determining the emotional state of a dog is the height or positioning of their tail.

For instance, a tail that is held parallel to the dog's back usually suggests that the dog is feeling relaxed, whereas, if the tail is held stiffly vertical, this usually means that the dog is feeling aggressive or dominant.

A tail held much lower can mean that the dog is feeling stressed, afraid, submissive or unwell and if the tail is tucked underneath the dog's body, this is most often a sign that the dog is feeling fearful and threatened by another dog or person.

Paying attention to your dog's tail can help you to know when you need to step in and make some space between your dog and another more dominant dog.

Of course, different breeds naturally carry their tails at different heights, so you will need to take this into consideration when studying your dog's tail so that you get used to their particular signals.

As well, the speed the tail is moving will also give you an idea of the mental state of the dog because the speed of the wag usually indicates how excited a dog may be.

For instance, a slow, slightly swinging wag can often mean that the dog is tentative about greeting another dog, and this is more of a questioning type of wag, whereas a fast moving tail held high can mean that a dog is about to challenge or threaten another less dominant dog.

Interestingly, two veterinarians at the University of Bari and a neuroscientist at the University of Trieste, in Italy, published a paper in which their research outlined that dogs' tails wagged more to their right side when they had positive feelings about a person or situation, and more to the left side when they were feeling negative.

While certainly a dog's tail can help us humans to understand how our dogs might be feeling, there are many other factors to take into consideration when determining your dog's state of mind.

Petting Definitely Works!

They don't refer to the Hungarian Vizsla as Velcro dogs for nothing. The easiest way to bond with your Hungarian Vizsla is to pet it. It is a language that your Vizsla understands well and will therefore be in a better position to reciprocate these emotions.

The Hungarian Vizsla is quite fond of laps. For the most part, whenever it finds you sitting peacefully in a corner, it will come around and sit in your lap to be petted. For the first few days, this behavior may seem to be absolutely lovable. However, keep in mind that if you over-shower your love and affection over the dog, it might create problems for you in future.

You can hug the Hungarian Vizsla, scratch its head or back, take it out for a walk or simply spend some time with it and it will readily grow on you. It is quite easy to help the Hungarian Vizsla settle down. All you need to do is be there when it needs you!

Chapter 10: Common Health Problems

Generally, all dogs are born healthy. A significant proportion of these are likely to lead perfectly healthy and fulfilling lives. A few of them may succumb to such miseries and die rather painful deaths. But it is important to note that such cases are few!

Much like all other dog breeds, the Hungarian Vizsla is prone to a couple of health complications. This may be attributed to cross breeding as was practiced during the conquests of Hungary. Nevertheless, it pays to keep an eye on these problems in order to lead a happy and healthy relationship with your pet!

Most of these problems may be averted through ethical breeding practices. If the breeder is making an effort to ensure the specimens used for procreation are healthy, there are slim chances for the young ones to develop any hereditary problems.

This is the reason why you are encouraged to take ample time in locating a genuine breeder. Anyone who has been involved with over two generations of Hungarian Vizslas will definitely know about the health complications typically faced by this breed. If the breeder says the breed is absolutely free from health risks, it is a sure sign of inexperience and trouble!

Here are some of the things you should be aware of in relation with your pet's health. The Hungarian Vizsla may prove to be a handful – in every sense!

1) Early Diagnosis

First things first; the Hungarian Vizsla is particularly prone to two diseases – the hip dysplasia and the progressive retinal atrophy. Of all the diseases that can affect the Hungarian Vizsla, the incidence of these medical conditions is particularly pronounced.

Both of these medical conditions are essentially hereditary in nature. For this reason, you are encouraged to conduct all kinds of checks in order to reach the authentic breeder. Ethical breeding practices can effectively put a stop to such problems. This is why it has been said time and again – with the right breeder, you have solved half of the equation!

The second thing you need to do before you head off to purchase your Hungarian Vizsla is this; ask for the parents' medical certificates. In particular, ask for clearance certificates from Orthopedic Foundation for Animals and from Canine Eye Registry Foundation. It is best if both parents score low on the risk factors. Even so, this cannot be considered as a guarantee that your pet will never fall ill. It merely reduces the risk instead of eliminating it altogether.

In most cases, you cannot recognize a hereditary disorder under the age of two years. Most of the symptoms start manifesting after you pet has reached of age. There is no conclusive way of identifying a threat before this time.

However, for the same reason, it is recommended not to breed Hungarian Vizslas before this age. If the parents are younger, their tests will not prove to be of any consequential worth. Hence, it will not help you or the breeder in screening these threats!

The specimen diagnosed with health problems shouldn't be allowed to mate. This is because these problems are then handed down several generations. Breeding healthy specimen can help reduce the risk of health complications in the next generations.

There's another popular problem with the Hungarian Vizsla. The Entropian is a medical condition in which the lower eyelid curls inwards in a way that irritates the eye balls. The eyelashes would continuously rub against the eye balls.

The Hungarian Vizsla may exhibit difficulty in viewing properly. This is one of those problems that you can identify in a Hungarian

Vizsla puppy just by looking at it. You don't need to put it through any diagnostic procedures to find out if it has Entropian problem.

The hip dysplasia is a problem in which the thighbone does not fit into the hip bone. This causes lameness in the rear part of its body. At times, the dog may experience moderate to excruciating pain while trying to use the joint. There is no solution to this problem. In most cases, the veterinary doctor will encourage you to put the dog to sleep in order to alleviate the condition.

Arthritis is also a natural follow up to this problem. Since the knee alignment will not be right, it will eventually cause aggravated wear and tear in the joints. This adds to the poor animal's miseries.

An X-Ray scan can usually identify the problem in the budding stage. Once your pet reaches the age of two, get it screened for hip dysplasia. Make sure the parents were certified clean of this problem. It all contributes towards the longevity of your pet.

Apart from this, the progressive retinal atrophy is another dangerous problem that may affect the Hungarian Vizsla. It is symbolized by progressive blindness. Although it doesn't really impact the life of the Hungarian Vizsla much, it nevertheless can be quite painful to get it accustomed to foreign environments. Usually though, dogs have the tendency to adapt to other senses in order to overcome the deficiency of one.

For the most part, the aforementioned conditions are untreatable. They become a lifelong handicap for your pet. To date there hasn't been a solution to these problems. The best policy is to keep away from these troubles through proper preliminary scans.

Apart from this, your Hungarian Vizsla may be prone to epilepsy, hypothyroidism, lymphosarcoma, Polymyositis, Sebaceous Adenitis, Atopic Dermatitis, Myasthenia Gravis, Hemophilia, and other similar problems. These problems may impact your dog's lifestyle moderately. The best way to go about this is to conduct regular screening sessions with the veterinary doctor.

Through proper and timely medication, the severity of these medical conditions can be controlled. For instance, it is possible to control epileptic seizures by administering the medicine regularly. The medicine helps in controlling the seizures. Though there is not permanent solution to the problem, it would nevertheless keep the apparent symptoms at bay as well!

With particular reference to this breed, the incidence of Polymyositis is on the rise. It is characterized by the inflammation of muscles that causes a change in the shape of its head. The dog will eventually begin to lose muscle. At severe stages, the pet may experience irreversible choking and subsequent death. The only solution for this problem is to identify it in a timely fashion. Once the disease has progressed beyond its initial phase, it is almost impossible to revert!

Hungarian Vizsla is a disease prone breed. This doesn't mean that every Hungarian Vizsla you choose will most definitely fall ill. It simply implies that the odds are high!

Ethical breeding practices can go a long way to curb uneventful incidences. You as the dog enthusiast need to play your unique and pivotal role in curbing such practices. In the long run, the gains are substantially more than the investment you make in terms of time and effort.

2) Shots, Vaccinations and Regular Check-Ups

One part of the problem lies in hereditary problems – your pet's proneness to contract a particular disease. The second half of the problem depends on how well you care for your pet.

The puppy receives the first antibodies in the form of the mother's milk. These friendly chemicals help the puppy adjust with the environment and to battle any infections or health problems that may occur during the transitory phase. It hardens the puppy to the surroundings so that it can lead an independent life.

However, once the puppy is put on an artificial diet other than the mother's milk, the inflow of antibodies stops. It makes it important for the puppy to receive these defensive particles from other sources. It is therefore recommended to provide the puppy with regular shots from the eighth week of its life.

Initially, the frequency of vaccinations is high – on a monthly basis. Over time, however, the frequency is reduced to once in every six months and then on to once a year. For older Hungarian Vizslas, the prescribed frequency is once every year.

Typically, the vaccinations given to the puppy during its lifetime include the famous DHLPP – shots for distemper, hepatitis, leptospirosis, parainfluenza, and parovirus. Some veterinary doctors encourage the use of a mega vaccine – the 5 in one shot that delivers all the necessary antibodies in one go. However, for very valid reasons, such a practice is not encouraged.

At times, dogs may exhibit allergic reactions to these vaccines. It is not the combination of different vaccines that add to the problem but rather a specific component of the vaccine. When these are administered in a single dose, it is impossible to pinpoint which vaccine might have caused the problem. In the worst-case scenario, this may end up in choking and subsequent death if medical help is not received in a timely fashion.

It is therefore recommended to give your dog the vaccines one at a time. If an allergic reaction is observed, make a mental note never to give the same vaccination again. Also, keep your pet under constant observation till you are absolutely confirmed there is nothing wrong with it.

Draft up a vaccination schedule in collaboration with the veterinary doctor. Make sure you don't miss out on any of these appointments. Also, take your puppy in for regular checkups. This will enable you to diagnose an imminent problem in a timely fashion.

Besides this, if your puppy requires medicine for any of its medical conditions, make sure you never miss out on these. The medicines cannot only help alleviate pain but also ensure longevity for your pet!

With the Hungarian Vizsla, you need to be a little more careful. It is a sensitive dog that is prone to a number of problems. Even if it is not about long drawn medical complications, regular health checks can help you give a quality life to your pet. It is all about the health and well-being of your pet – the healthier it is, the happier you will be!

Chapter 11: Caring for Your Hungarian Vizsla

You are now aware of all the things that influence your decision to purchase a Hungarian Vizsla. From its personality and temperament to its specific characteristics and proneness to health issues, the Hungarian Vizsla is unique in every sense. So if you've decided to bring one home, it is now time to work on other pet needs.

For the most part, Hungarian Vizslas make great companions. They are intelligent dogs that are easy to train. They won't prove to be very challenging. Yet there are some aspects of its grooming that you need to pay specific focus to.

This section talks about how you can care for your Hungarian Vizsla in the best possible manner. Keep in mind that the dog (any breed for that matter) is just another animal. Even though most dogs are intelligent self-learners, you shouldn't expect them to take care of themselves. They are naïve and innocent – you'll have to care for them as you would for someone of your own kind!

1) Its Grooming Concerns

Did you ever see a dog that wouldn't mess around, wouldn't try to explore corners and would simply not get its paws dirty? Well, no one has! Such a specimen has yet to be found! This inevitably means that you need to groom your pet from time to time regardless of which breed it is!

Here are some grooming tips for your pet that will help you keep your Hungarian Vizsla presentable at all times. It sure is difficult but not entirely impossible! Keep in mind that its grooming is inescapably linked with its health concerns. So you need to be a little active this end to give your pet the life it deserves!

a. Its Coat

The Hungarian Vizsla has an extremely short coat. Moreover, it does not have an undercoat. Most experts believe the Hungarian Vizsla breed does not shed. However, if you seem to notice any uncanny short hairs sticking on your furniture, don't worry. Although it doesn't shed heavily, it is normal for the Hungarian Vizsla to shed some hair from time to time.

As far as its grooming needs are concerned, you'll need to brush its coat regularly – preferably on a daily basis. Since it does not have a lot of hair on its coat, this will not prove to be much of a problem for you. In addition to the apparent improvement of looks, brushing the coat regularly also stimulates blood flow towards the skin. This in turn contributes towards a healthy coat.

Brushing also helps you bond with your Hungarian Vizsla. Seeing that it is a Velcro dog who likes being pampered by their human masters, this would be seen as an attempt to bond. So while it definitely plays a role in improving the outlook of the Hungarian Vizsla, it will also provide other unparalleled benefits.

Keep in mind that, at any given point of time, if you observe any noticeable changes in the Vizsla's coat call in for immediate consultation.

Sebaceous Adenitis tends to begin with extremely subtle symptoms. Your veterinary doctor will be in a better state to diagnose the problem in the initial stages. If the veterinary doctor diagnoses a problem with your pet, make sure you follow through the prescription carefully.

b. Its Nails

The second most important part of the Hungarian Vizsla's grooming is to have its nails done. There are a couple of dog parlors that will be willing to take your pet in for some personalized care. Nevertheless, you can do the same at home as well. It gives you another opportunity to bond with your Hungarian Vizsla dog.

With the nails, the most precarious part of the activity is to determine how short to trim them. Leaving the nails too long can cause you a lot of pain as the Hungarian Vizsla tries to hold on to you. Besides this, long nails can cause a problem with gait as well.

Out in their natural habitat, their hunting instincts cause the nails to get worn out. This is one reason the nails do not grow too long. But when you are caring for the pet at home, you'll need to do the chore yourself.

Make sure you do not cut the nails too short or the dog will be in a lot of pain. Naturally, the pink part of the paw is the must-avoid. Take your time to trim your puppy's nails – don't be in a rush – to avoid accidents. Moreover, it is advised to have some help during the nail trimming process. This will help you keep the puppy's paw steady so you don't end up cutting more than the nail.

You can use nail trimmers as well. This saves you from the risk of cutting your puppy's nails. It'll be a good idea to invest in a high quality dog nail trimmer – you'll be using this equipment quite often. Even so, make sure you are not trimming the pink part of the puppy's paw!

For the Hungarian Vizsla in particular, it is advised to use a puppy paw balm. It helps prevent cracks and dryness of the skin. Given the absence of an undercoat and the presence of a short overcoat, the use of puppy paw balm becomes necessary during the dry winter months!

c. Dental Hygiene

Dental hygiene applies to your puppy as much as it applies to you. Make sure you get it into a habit of regular brushing earlier on in life. This will save you from quite a few tantrums later on.

Here's a food for thought; is your puppy's teeth really the area you'd like to be close to while it is resisting your efforts to groom it? Better get it accustomed to the chore while its jaws are incapable of hurting you!

You can either use nylon cloth for this purpose or use a child's toothbrush. Make sure the material is soft and does not hurt the gums. Use commercially produced dog toothpastes to produce one yourself. Keep in mind that your pet's dental health is intricately related with its overall health. Invest your time and effort wisely in order to maximize your returns!

Regular brushing helps in preventing halitosis – a bad breath problem particular to dogs. Unless you can keep up with intolerant odors, you might want to try brushing your puppy's teeth daily!

d. Its Ears

It's the same for all dog breeds; you need to get them checked regularly for ear infections and other similar problems. Ear cropping does not help prevent infections – contrary to what most people believe. Make sure you take your puppy in for regular checkups!

Moreover, take some time to remove the debris from your puppy's ears manually. You need to be extra careful while doing this because you don't want to hurt its inner lobes. Take some cotton buds to help you clean out its ears. This becomes exceptionally important once your puppy has had its periodic bath.

If you observe any unexplained debris or discharges from the Hungarian Vizsla's ears, seek medical help immediately. It is not normal for your puppy, and as the owner, it is your responsibility to find out why it is happening so!

Last but not the least; never use commercially produced concoctions for cleaning your puppy's ears without prior consultation from the veterinary doctor. Don't believe the labels – they are there to get your attention. Before using chemicals on your pet, make sure they have been declared safe.

e. Its Eyes

It is priceless to see your puppy's eye light up with excitement when they see you after a long day. You need to protect its eyes in order to retain the shine.

While bathing your pet, make sure you do not let the soap enter its eyes. For the most part, soaps may irritate its eyes. Secondly, it is not meant to be there. You can clean its face and muzzle with water if you want but you need to make sure its eyes are kept dry.

It is normal for debris to build up in the eyes of your dog. Use a soft cloth dampened with warm water to clean out the debris. Keep all sharp objects and surfaces away from its eyes.

If the debris is not cleared in time, it may lead to bigger problems like yeast infections. In any case, the debris may cause the eye lids to get glued together. So your puppy will face unnecessary trouble in viewing. A little effort on your part can help your pet enormously!

f. Bathing

It is a fun activity for your pet as well as for you. The only problem is this; most dogs are averse to water. So it might take some extra effort to get your puppy accustomed to water and bathing routines. Here's a step by step guide to bathe your

Hungarian Vizsla. It would minimize the resistance put forth by your pet!

Step One: Before you get your Hungarian Vizsla anywhere near the water, it's important to make sure that you brush out any debris, or dead hair from their coat before you begin the bathing process.

As well, removing any debris from your dog's coat beforehand will make the entire process easier on you, your dog, and your drains, which will become clogged with dead hair if you don't remove it beforehand.

Step Two: Since your Hungarian Vizsla does not have a long coat, you wouldn't need to spray a light mist of leave-in conditioner before brushing. Nevertheless, doing so will help soften up its coarse and brittle hair so that the dead ones can be removed easily!

Step Three: Whether you're bathing your Hungarian Vizsla in your laundry tub, bathtub or sink, you will always want to first lay down a rubber bath mat to provide a more secure footing for your dog and to prevent your tub or sink from being scratched.

Step Four: Have everything you need for the bath (shampoo, conditioner, sponge, towels) right next to the sink or tub, so you don't have to go searching once your dog is already in the water. It's a Velcro dog; it will most probably follow you around the house to fetch the products. Unless you've got no issues with wet soapy trails, you'll be better off having everything nearby when you get started!

Place cotton balls in your Hungarian Vizsla dog's ear canals to prevent accidental splashes from entering the ear canal that could later cause an ear infection. Even so, it is good idea to dry the ear later on – just in case!

Step Five: Fill the tub or sink with four to six inches of lukewarm water (not too hot as dogs are more sensitive to hot water than us humans) and put your Hungarian Vizsla dog in the water. Completely wet your dog's coat right down to the skin by using a detachable showerhead. If you don't have a spray attachment, a cup or pitcher will work just as well.

Rub your fingers between the hairs to make sure water reaches the skin. The Hungarian Vizsla likes being stroked so you needn't worry about offending it.

Step Six: Apply shampoo as indicated on the bottle instructions by beginning at the head and working your way down the back. Be careful not to get shampoo in the eyes, nose, mouth, or ears. Comb the shampoo lather through your dog's hair with your fingers, making sure you don't miss the areas under the legs and the tail.

Step Seven: After allowing the shampoo to remain in your dog's coat for a couple of minutes, thoroughly rinse the Hungarian Vizsla dog's coat, right down to the skin with clean, lukewarm water using the spray attachment, cup or pitcher. Comb through your dog's coat with your fingers to make sure all shampoo residues has been completely rinsed away.

Any shampoo remaining in a dog's coat will lead to irritation and itching. Once you've rinsed, take the time to rinse again, especially in the armpits and underneath the tail area.

Use your hands to gently squeeze all excess water from your dog's coat.

Step Eight: Apply conditioner as indicated on the bottle instructions and work the conditioner throughout your dog's coat. Leave the conditioner in your dog's coat for two minutes and then thoroughly rinse again with warm water, unless the conditioner you are using is a *"leave-in"*, no-rinse formula.

The best conditioner for a Hungarian Vizsla will contain mink oil, which adds a gloss to deepen and enrich the natural color of the coat.

It is also a good idea to choose a brand of conditioner that contains sunscreen to help protect from ultraviolet radiation when your dog is outside on sunny days.

Applying a good conditioner containing protein to your Hungarian Vizsla dog's coat after bathing will help to rebuild, restructure, and protect the coat by bonding to the shaft of each individual hair.

Pull the plug on your sink or tub and let the water drain away as you use your hands to squeeze excess water from your Hungarian Vizsla dog's legs and feet.

Step Nine: Immediately out of the water, wrap your Hungarian Vizsla in dry towels so they don't get cold and use the towels to gently squeeze out extra water before you allow them to shake and spray water everywhere.

Dry your Hungarian Vizsla further with your hand held hairdryer and be careful not to let the hot air get too close to their skin.

Place your hand between the hairdryer and your Hungarian Vizsla dog's hair so that they will never get a direct blast of hot air and never blow air directly into their face or ears.

Don't forget to remove the cotton balls from their ears!

Keep asides at least 30minutes of your time for this task. Your Hungarian Vizsla might be prone to playfulness during the bathe. Bear with it; it is only trying to impress you!

g. Brushing and Combing

The Hungarian Vizsla does not have a lot of hair. But whatever hair it does have, you'd want to brush these regularly in order to prevent hair fall and heavy shedding.

Use a soft bristled brush (preferably made from an organic source) to comb your Hungarian Vizsla's coat. It is a good idea to have a couple of brushes placed strategically across the house. This will save you from the trouble of fetching one if you have your pet lying cozily nearby.

Spend at least 15 to 20 minutes at this task. Brush its head and back nicely. The purpose is not to free any tangles but to stimulate the flow of blood towards the skin. This, in turn, makes the coat shiny and healthy.

Brushing also helps you get rid of dead hair, which may get logged in your furniture. You need to be brushing your pet's coat at least twice a week if not every day. If you Hungarian Vizsla dog look presentable and healthy, it says a lot about the kind of master you are!

2) Feeding Concerns

Grooming the Hungarian Vizsla is not much of a challenge. It takes about half an hour of your day to keep your Hungarian Vizsla in a perfectly presentable state. If you've got this part of the equation under control, there is little you need to worry about!

The next most important thing for you to consider is its feeding routines. What will the Hungarian Vizsla eat? How much will it eat? How often will it dine? It depends on the age of your pet. This section will talk about your Hungarian Vizsla's dog food in detail!

For the Hungarian Vizsla, providing high quality dog food is imperative. It cannot thrive on poor quality food. Because of its thin coat and absence of an undercoat, every ounce that your pet gains or loses becomes evident immediately. So you need to be extra careful about what or how much you are feeding your pet!

Fortunately or unfortunately, Hungarian Vizslas are choosy about their food. This means you might need to experiment with several different kinds of dog foods before you can find the one that suits your pet. Especially in this situation, make a mental note about the kind of dog food your pet was being given at the breeders. It will help you get through the first few days and weeks easily.

This breed is known to be lean and well-muscled without a lot of fats. A healthy Hungarian Vizsla is considered to be the one who doesn't show the spinal column or the ribs while standing in the relaxed position. However, when it bends, slight appearance of the skeletal system is considered normal and healthy!

a. Feeding Young Hungarian Vizsla Dogs

The young ones thrive on the mother's milk for up to a period of two months. It receives its nutrition as well as antibodies from the mother. This phase is extremely crucial for your pet. So don't deprive it of its basic right!

After the eighth week, the breeder will try to shift the dog from the mother's milk to dog foods. The transition is extremely slow. During this period, the dog is increasingly being introduced to solid diet. The frequency of mother's feeding will decrease proportionately with the increase of solid dog food. This is done to ensure that the puppy's health is not affected.

This transitory phase may last for up to four weeks. After this time period, the puppy will shift completely to dog food. The Hungarian Vizsla requires high quality and high protein dog food. For the most part, it does not tolerate cereal based dog foods.

At this time, the puppy will be given several small servings of dog food per day. Ideally, your Hungarian Vizsla will need four

50-75 gram servings in a day. At this time, the water content in the dog food needs to be high. This enables the puppy to digest the food efficiently.

As the puppy hits the six month mark, the frequency of feeding will decrease while the serving size increases. For instance, instead of providing it food four times a day, you'll be giving it roughly 100 gram servings three times a day. As your puppy grows in size, you'll need to increase its serving size accordingly.

The second most important determinant of its serving size is its activity levels. If you puppy is hyperactive, or if you are exercising it daily, you'll need to feed it high quantities of dog food to compromise for the energy lost. Conversely, if you are unable to exercise your puppy, you might want to feed it smaller servings to compromise for the excess energy.

By the end of the first year, you should have reduced the serving frequency to twice a day. The serving size may be anywhere between 100 and 300 grams of dog food. Also, at this time, you don't need to add a lot of water to its food. The dog's digestive system will gradually learn to work with solid dog food.

Use premium dog foods only. Your Hungarian Vizsla needs a lot of proteins in order to build muscles and sustain a better health. Investing in poor quality dog food will not only impact your Hungarian Vizsla's health but also make it prone to a number of growth related disorders.

b. Feeding Adult Hungarian Vizsla Dogs

As the Hungarian Vizsla grows older, its requirements change. For instance, beyond the second year of the Hungarian Vizsla's life, the purpose of the feeding is not to grow but rather to sustain. Most of the energy will now be directed towards internal and external maintenance. A two year old Hungarian Vizsla is considered to have matured!

Ideally, an adult Hungarian Vizsla consumes food twice a day. The serving size will depend on its activity levels. For hyperactive pets, you might want to apportion higher quantities of food in a given serving time.

On this note, beware of free feeding. Don't leave the food bowls lying around all day. You need to discipline your pet from day one. If you accustom your pet to free feeding, it will lead to personality disorders later on.

Set a time frame in which your puppy will be allowed to feed. For instance, leave the bowls out for one hour. Make sure you instruct your pet to consume it once you lay it out. But if it doesn't eat much by the end of the hour, remove the bowl nevertheless. This will help in disciplining your pet!

Free feeding makes the Hungarian Vizsla believe it is the leader. It will feed whenever it feels like. You need to inhibit such symptoms beforehand to make sure your pet understands who the real master is!

It is also a good idea not to let your Hungarian Vizsla feast beyond 8 in the evening. Usually, your Hungarian Vizsla will experience the call of nature within two to three hours of feeding. Unless you are comfortable escorting your pet outdoors in the middle of the night, you'd restrict its food intake beyond this time.

Regardless of your Hungarian Vizsla's age, you need to be extremely particular about the quality of food you feed to your pet. It is extremely imperative for you to be choosy about your pet's diet. Seek the veterinary doctor's advice about what to feed your pet.

You might need to give your Hungarian Vizsla certain supplements in order to bridge the gap in its nutritional requirements. This becomes more pronounced if your pet is choosy about its food. Don't use any supplements without consulting the vet first! The rest should be fine!

c. Frequency of Feeding

How frequently or how much should you feed your Hungarian Vizsla depends on its activity levels. For a hyperactive Hungarian Vizsla dog, you'll need to serve large servings. The ideal feeding frequency for an adult Hungarian Vizsla is twice in a day. But when they are younger, you'll need to feed them small quantities more often to make up for their nutritional requirements.

Start your puppy on a 4 – 5 times in a day diet. Slowly reduce the number of servings and increase the serving size. The process can take up to 1 year to complete. When it is down to two sizeable servings in a day, you can be rest assured it is ideal for your pet.

Never allow your pet to feed freely. Free feeding gives rise to behavioral problems and other complications. Develop a feeding schedule for your pet and stick to it – it is for your pet's own good!

d. Treats

Since the creation of the first dog treat over 150 years ago the myriad of choices available on every pet store, feed store and grocery store shelf almost outnumbers those looking forward to eating them.

Today's treats are not just for making us guilty humans feel better because it makes us happy to give our fur friends something they really enjoy because today's treats are also designed to actually improve our dog's health.

Some of us humans treat our dogs for no particular reason; others use treats for training purposes; some others for health, while still others treat for a combination of reasons.

Whatever reason you choose to give treats to your Hungarian Vizsla, keep in mind that if we treat our dogs too often throughout the day, we may create a picky eater who will no longer want to eat their regular meals. Seeing that Hungarian is already one, this will only make matters worse for you!

As well, if the treats we are giving are high calorie, we may be putting our dog's health in jeopardy by allowing them to become overweight. Your Hungarian Vizsla doesn't need as much calories as it needs a balanced protein-rich diet!

e. Healthy Treats

Here are a few healthy treats that you can treat your Hungarian Vizsla with!

Hard Treats

There are so many choices of hard or crunchy treats available that come in many varieties of shapes, sizes and flavors, that you may have a difficult time choosing.

If your Hungarian Vizsla will eat them, hard treats will help to keep their teeth cleaner.

Whatever you do choose, be certain to read the labels and make sure that the ingredients are high quality and appropriately sized for your Hungarian Vizsla friend.

Soft Treats

Soft, chewy treats are also available in a wide variety of flavors, shapes and sizes for all the different needs of our hairy and furry friends and are often used for training purposes as they have a stronger smell.

Dental Treats

Dental treats or chews are designed with the specific purpose of helping your Hungarian Vizsla to maintain healthy teeth and gums.

They usually require intensive chewing and are often shaped with high ridges and bumps to exercise the jaw and massage gums while removing plaque build-up near the gum line.

Freeze-Dried and Jerky Treats

Freeze-dried and jerky treats offer a tasty morsel most dogs find irresistible as they are usually made of simple, meaty ingredients, such as liver, poultry and seafood.

These treats are usually lightweight and easy to carry around, which means they can also be great as training treats.

Human Food Treats

You will want to be very careful when feeding human foods to dogs as treats, because many of our foods contain additives and ingredients that could be toxic and harmful.

Be certain to choose simple, fresh foods with minimal or no processing, such as lean meat, poultry or seafood, and even if your Hungarian Vizsla will not really eat anything put in front of them, be aware that many common human foods, such as grapes, raisins, onions and chocolate are poisonous to dogs.

Training Treats

While any sort of treat can be used as an extra incentive during training sessions, soft treats are often used for training purposes because of their stronger smell and smaller sizes.

Yes, we humans love to treat our dogs, whether for helping to teach the new puppy to go pee outside, teaching the adolescent dog new commands, for trick training, for general good behavior, or for no reason at all, other than that they just gave us the *"look"*.

Generally, the treats you feed your dog should not make up more than approximately 10% of their daily food intake. Make sure the treats you choose are high quality so that you can help to keep your Hungarian Vizsla both happy and healthy.

f. Harmful Treats

Not all treats are healthy for your puppy's consumption. Here are a few harmful treats you should be aware of. Eliminate these from your shopping list to ensure a long and happy life for your Hungarian Vizsla puppy!

Rawhide

Rawhide is soaked in an ash/lye solution to remove every particle of meat, fat and hair and then further soaked in bleach to remove remaining traces of the ash/lye solution. Now that the product is no longer food, it no longer has to comply with food regulations.

While the hide is still wet it is shaped into rawhide chews, and upon drying it shrinks to approximately 1/4 of its original size.

Further, arsenic based products are often used as preservatives, and antibiotics and insecticides are added to kill bacteria that also fight against good bacteria in your dog's intestines.

The collagen fibers in the rawhide make it very tough and long lasting which makes this chew a popular choice for humans to give to their dogs because it satisfies the dog's natural urge to chew while providing many hours of quiet entertainment.

Sadly, when a dog chews a rawhide treat, they ingest many harsh chemicals and when your dog swallows a piece of rawhide, that piece can swell up to four times its normal size inside your dog's stomach, which can cause anything from mild to severe gastric blockages that could become life threatening and require surgery.

Pig Ears

These treats are actually the ears of pigs, and while most dogs will eagerly devour them, they are extremely high in fat, which can cause stomach upsets, vomiting and diarrhea for many dogs.

Pig ears are often processed and preserved with unhealthy chemicals that discerning dog guardians will not want to feed their dogs.

As well, the ears are often quite thin and crispy and when the dog chews them pieces can break off, like chips, and can easily become stuck in a dog's throat.

While pig ears are generally not considered to be a healthy treat choice for any dog, they should be especially avoided for any dog that may be at risk of being overweight.

Hoof Treats

Many humans give cow, horse and pig hooves to their dogs as treats because they consider them to be *"natural"*.

The truth is that after processing these *"treats"* they retain little, if any, of their *"natural"* qualities.

Hoof treats are processed with harsh preservatives, including insecticides, lead, bleach, arsenic based products, and antibiotics to kill bacteria, that can also harm the good bacteria in your dog's intestines, and if all bacteria is not killed in these meat based products before feeding them to your dog, they could also suffer from Salmonella poisoning.

Hooves can also cause chipping or breaking of your dog's teeth as well as perforation or blockages in your dog's intestines.

g. Choosing the Right Food

In order to choose the right food for your Hungarian Vizsla, first, it's important to understand a little bit about canine physiology and what Mother Nature intended when she created our fur friends.

More than 230 years ago, in 1785, the English Sportman's dictionary described the best diet for a dog's health in an article entitled *"Dog"*.

This article indicated that the best food for a dog was something called *"Greaves"*, described as *"the sediment of melted tallow. It is made into cakes for dogs' food. In Scotland and parts of the US it is called cracklings."*

Out of the meager beginning of the first commercially made dog food has sprung a massively lucrative and vastly confusing industry that has only recently begun to evolve beyond those early days of feeding our dogs the dregs of human leftovers because it was cheap and convenient for us humans.

Even today, the majority of dog food choices have far more to do with being convenient for humans to store and serve than it does with being a diet truly designed to be a nutritionally balanced, healthy food choice for a canine.

The dog food industry is big business and as such, because there are now almost limitless choices, there is much confusion and endless debate when it comes to answering the question, *"What is the best food for my dog?"*

Educating yourself, by talking to experts and reading everything you can find on the subject, plus taking into consideration several relevant factors, will help to answer the dog food question for you and your dog.

For instance, where you live may dictate what sorts of foods you have access to. Other factors to consider will include the particular requirements of your dog, such as their age, energy and activity levels.

Next will be expense, time and quality. While we all want to give our dogs the best food possible, many humans lead very busy lives and cannot, for instance, prepare their own dog food, but still want to feed a high quality diet that fits within their budget.

However, perhaps most important when choosing an appropriate diet for our dogs, is learning to be more observant of Mother Nature's design and taking a closer look at our dog's teeth, jaws and digestive tract. While humans are herbivores who derive energy from eating plants, our canine companions are carnivores, which means that they derive their energy and nutrient requirements from eating a diet consisting mainly or exclusively of the flesh of animal tissues (in other words, meat).

The Canine Teeth

The first part of your dog you will want to take a good look at when considering what to feed will be their teeth. Unlike humans, who are equipped with wide, flat molars for grinding grains, vegetables and other plant-based materials, canine teeth are all pointed because they are designed to rip, shred and tear into animal meat and bone.

The Canine Jaw

Another obvious consideration when choosing an appropriate food source for our fur friends is the fact that every canine is born equipped with powerful jaws and neck muscles for the specific purpose of being able to pull down and tear apart their hunted prey. The structure of the jaw of every canine is such that it opens widely to hold large pieces of meat and bone, while the actual mechanics of a dog's jaw permits only vertical (up and down) movement that is designed for crushing.

The Canine Digestive Tract

A dog's digestive tract is short and simple and designed to move their natural choice of food (hide, meat and bone) quickly through their systems.

Vegetables and plant matter require more time to break down in the gastrointestinal tract, which in turn, requires a more complex digestive system than the canine body is equipped with.

The canine digestive system is simply unable to break down vegetable matter, which is why whole vegetables look pretty much the same going into your dog as they do coming out the other end.

Given the choice, most dogs would never choose to eat plants or vegetables and fruits over meat; however, we humans continue to feed them a kibble based diet that contains high amounts of vegetables, fruits and grains and low amounts of meat.

Plus, in order to get our dogs to eat fruits, vegetables and grains we usually have to flavor the food with meat or meat by-products.

How much healthier and long lived might our beloved fur friends will be if, instead of largely ignoring nature's design for our canine companions, we chose to feed them whole, unprocessed, species-appropriate food?

With many hundreds of dog food brands to choose from, it's no wonder we humans are confused about what to feed our dogs to help them live long and healthy lives.

Following are some suggestions and questions that may help you choose a dog food company that you can feel comfortable with:

- How long have they have been in business?
- Is dog food their main industry?
- Are they dedicated to their brand?

- Are they easily accessible?
- Do they honestly answer your questions?
- Do they have a good Company Safety Standard?
- Do they set higher standards?
- Read the ingredients - where did they come from?
- Are the ingredients something you would eat?
- Are the ingredients farmed locally?
- Was it cooked using standards you would trust?
- Is the company certified under human food or organic guidelines?

Whatever you decide to feed your Hungarian Vizsla dog, keep in mind that just as too much wheat, other grains and other fillers in our human diet is having detrimental effects on our human health, the same can be very true for our best fur friends.

Our dogs are also suffering from many of the same life threatening diseases that are rampant in our human society (heart disease, cancer) as a direct result of consuming a diet high in genetically altered, impure, processed and packaged foods.

h. The Raw Diet

While some of us believe we are killing ourselves as well as our dogs with processed foods, others believe that there are dangers in feeding raw foods.

Those who are raw feeding advocates believe that the ideal diet for their dog is one which would be very similar to what a dog living in the wild would have access to hunting or foraging, and these canine guardians are often opposed to feeding their dog any sort of commercially manufactured pet foods, because they consider them to be poor substitutes.

On the other hand, those opposed to feeding their dogs a raw or biologically appropriate raw food diet, believe that the risks associated with food-borne illnesses during the handling and feeding of raw meats outweigh the purported benefits.

Interestingly, even though the United States Food and Drug Administration (FDA) states that they do not advocate a raw diet for dogs, they do advise for those who wish to take this route, that following basic hygiene guidelines for handling raw meat can minimize any associated risks.

Further, high pressure pasteurization (HPP), which is high pressure, water based technology for killing bacteria, is USDA-approved for use on organic and natural food products, and is being utilized by many commercial raw pet food manufacturers.

Interestingly, raw meats purchased at your local grocery store contain a much higher level of acceptable bacteria than raw food produced for dogs because the meat purchased for human consumption is supposed to be cooked, which will kill any bacteria that might be present.

This means that canine guardians feeding their dogs a raw food diet can be quite certain that commercially prepared raw foods sold in pet stores will be safer than raw meats purchased in grocery stores.

Many guardians of high energy, working breed dogs will agree that their dogs thrive on a raw or BARF (Biologically Appropriate Raw Food) diet and strongly believe that the potential benefits of feeding a raw dog food diet are many, including:

- healthy, shiny coats
- decreased shedding
- fewer allergy problems
- healthier skin
- cleaner teeth
- fresher breath
- higher energy levels
- improved digestion
- smaller stools

- strengthened immune system
- increased mobility in arthritic pets
- increase or improvement in overall health

All dogs, of every size, whether working breed or companion dogs are amazing athletes in their own right. Therefore every dog deserves to be fed the best food available.

A raw diet is a direct evolution of what dogs ate before they became our domesticated pets and we turned toward commercially prepared, easy to serve dry dog food that required no special storage or preparation.

The BARF diet is all about feeding our dogs what they are designed to eat by returning them to their wild, evolutionary diet.

i. The Dehydrated Diet

Dehydrated dog food comes in both raw meat and cooked meat forms and these foods are usually air dried to reduce moisture to the level where bacterial growth is inhibited.

The appearance of de-hydrated dog food is very similar to dry kibble and the typical feeding methods include adding warm water before serving, which makes this type of diet both healthy for our dogs and convenient for us to serve.

Dehydrated recipes are made from minimally processed fresh whole foods to create a healthy and nutritionally balanced meal that will meet or exceed the dietary requirements of a healthy canine. Dehydrating removes only the moisture from the fresh ingredients, which usually means that because the food has not already been cooked at a high temperature, more of the overall nutrition is retained.

A dehydrated diet is a convenient way to feed your dog a nutritious diet because all you have to do is add warm water, and wait five minutes while the food rehydrates so your Hungarian Vizsla can enjoy a warm meal.

j. The Kibble Diet

While many canine guardians are starting to take a closer look at the food choices they are making for their furry companions, there is no mistaking that the convenience and relative economy of dry dog food kibble, that had its beginnings in the 1940's, continues to be the most popular pet food choice for most dog friendly humans.

Some 75 years later, the massive pet food industry offers up a confusingly large number of choices with hundreds of different manufacturers and brand names lining the shelves of veterinarian offices, grocery stores and pet food aisles.

While feeding a high quality bagged kibble diet that has been flavored to appeal to dogs and supplemented with vegetables and fruits to appeal to humans, may keep almost every Hungarian Vizsla companion happy and relatively healthy, you will ultimately need to decide whether this is the best diet for them.

k. The Right Feeding Bowl

Following is a brief description of the different categories and types of dog bowls that would be appropriate choices for your Hungarian Vizsla's particular needs.

Automatic Watering Bowls are standard dog bowls (often made out of plastic) that are attached to a reservoir container. They are designed to keep water constantly available to your dog as long as there is water supply in the storage compartment.

Ceramic/Stoneware Bowls are an excellent choice for those who like options in personality, color and shape.

Elevated Bowls are raised dining table dog bowls that are a tidy and classy choice. It will make your dog's dinner time a more comfortable experience while getting the bowls off the floor.

No Skid Bowls are for dogs that push their bowls across the floor when eating. A non-skid dog bowl will help keep the feed bowl where you put it.

No Tip Bowls are designed to prevent the messy type of doggy eater from flipping over their dinner or water bowls.

Stainless Steel Bowls are as close to indestructible as a bowl can possibly be! Plus they are sanitary, easy to clean and water stays cooler for a longer period of time in a stainless bowl.

Wooden Bowls are for those humans concerned about stylish home décor. Wooden dog bowl dining stations are beautiful pieces of furniture in themselves that can enhance your home decor.

Travel Bowls are convenient, practical and handy additions for every canine travel kit.

Consider a space saving, collapsible dog bowl made out of hygienic, renewable bamboo that comes in fun colors and different sizes; making it perfect for every travel bowl needs.

If you would like to learn more about all the many dog bowl choices available, visit DogBowlForYourDog.com, which is a comprehensive, one-stop website dedicated to explaining the ins and outs of every food bowl imaginable and helping you find the perfect bowl for all your Hungarian Vizsla's needs.

3) Accommodating the Hungarian Vizsla

The Hungarian Vizsla is strictly an indoor companion dog. If you are hoping to put it to guarding duties around the house, you'll face extreme disappointment. This is one reason why you are encouraged to take your time before you decide to bring a puppy in.

Different dog breeds are suited for different roles. Discuss to find out which dog breeds should you adopt – something good will definitely come of it.

Don't be under the illusion that a puppy/dog does not occupy any space. They mature readily – the Hungarian Vizsla grows to its fullest by the end of its second year. It is a medium sized dog and definitely occupies space.

Besides its apparent size, you will need to accommodate its needs. For instance, you'll have to provide a dedicated sleeping area, an exercise pen and other similar needs. Here is a little insight about its specific special needs you will need to make place for!

a. Its Sleep Area

Generally, all dogs like having a dedicated space for their sleep. This means a separate room or a specific corner of your house. Also, it is best if it is a secluded and silent spot. If you design the Hungarian Vizsla dog's sleep area in the middle of commotion, rest assured it will not be able to sleep. Instead, it will jump up to the occasion and start playing around with you every time you pass by its sleep area.

Keep in mind never to let the Hungarian Vizsla dog sleep with you in your bed. By doing so, you will end up reinforcing negative habits and traits in your Hungarian Vizsla dog. It will begin considering itself to be the leader of the "pack" and will therefore become a challenge to maintain. Define the boundaries for your pet while you still can.

b. Exercise Area

Hungarian Vizsla is a medium sized dog and therefore will have some (if not a lot) built up energy resource that needs to be expended. A daily walk around a park or in the streets suffices to provide for its exercise needs. However, make sure you are not carrying it in your arms or letting it trot by your side without a leash. The former case kills the purpose of the walk altogether and the latter one accentuates the probability of an escape.

Familiarize your Hungarian Vizsla with the neighborhood during the first few weeks. This will ensure your Hungarian Vizsla is able to find its way back if and when it makes a dash into the wilderness. However, never let it off the leash. The cute and amiable appearance of the Hungarian Vizsla can be dissolved in minutes if the dog feels threatened.

Take it for a walk on a daily basis and make sure you include a weekly or monthly hike in its exercise routine as well. This will not only keep your puppy fit and healthy but also work just the same for you!

c. Play Area

This is the area where your puppy will spend most of its time getting entertained by mindless activities. It is also the place where you will most probably be leaving the puppy without active supervision. It is therefore a natural instinct to puppy-proof this area to the best of your capacity.

Clear the room of all "human" furniture. It'll be a good idea to install a fixed carpet in this room to provide greater stability for its feet. Add in a few toys to this room that your pet likes and is unlikely to choke on and you are done! If there are any windows or doors in the room, make sure you install adequate barriers to keep the puppy in as once it gets bored, it will try to get out and explore "the world beyond"!

Mazes and obstacle courses can stimulate your pet's mind and facilitate its physical as well as mental development. Make sure you invest in your dog's toys wisely – it will define how your pet will look years down the line!

d. Socialization Arena

The Hungarian Vizsla – seeing that it is popularly known as a Velcro dog – can be safely regarded as a social dog. It usually greets strangers in a warm manner – which poses a question to its guarding capabilities. Nevertheless, you wouldn't need to invest heavily to get your pet accustomed to the city life.

For this dog, walks in parks and gathering at your home will be sufficient to make it sociable and amiable. If you have any doubts about your pet's behavior, put it on a leash and keep it at a safe distance from other people. Keep it vaccinated regularly to minimize damages in case of an accident. The rest should be fine.

4) Traveling Concerns

Travel crates are easily the best option available to transport your pet. Make sure it has ample space inside to move a little. Hungarian Vizsla dogs, seeing their size, will adjust easily with the travel crates. Alternatively, the next best option for you is to employ your personal car!

Public transport, though not really prohibited, will not be a very good idea considering its Velcro nature. If the place is not too far away, try walking your canine companion to its destination – it will be able to get its daily dose of exercise. If this isn't possible, avoid putting other people's lives in danger and use your car instead!

Your car might need a few adjustments to accommodate your pet. Nevertheless, it is an investment worth making – especially if you are a frequent traveler!

Remember to add in identification documents to your dog's collar before leaving home and put it on a leash wherever possible. Keep the windows rolled up so your Hungarian Vizsla does not feel the impulse to escape.

Also, try to keep it on the back seat to prevent it from interfering with your driving. The ideal scenario is to have someone holding the dog and keeping it distracted.

Hungarian Vizsla dogs might get excited by movement. So naturally, having blinds or some toys to keep its eyes away from the windows will be a good idea!

Also, know how your pet signals the call of nature. You definitely do not want reminders of the trip in your car.

Take frequent breaks and walk the Hungarian Vizsla dog to exhaust its energy reserves. A tired Hungarian Vizsla is easier to control as compared with one that is full of energy. Improvise along the way as and when required.

There are no hard and fast principles – go with your gut instincts and you should be fine!

After the first few visits, you will automatically find out what more needs to be done to facilitate travels. It isn't a one-time affair. So we suggest you adapt to the rising needs with time!

5) Daily Grooming Guidelines

The Hungarian Vizsla is a relatively non-hairy breed. It does not have long hairs that are prone to get tangled if not brushed regularly. It is therefore easier to groom a Hungarian Vizsla. Brushing its coat once or twice in a day should be sufficient.

The best way is to keep a hair brush in every room where you spend time with your pet. Once it gets busy playing with you or exhibiting its affection for you, just grab the brush and comb its hair. If you have to get up to fetch a brush, it will definitely become a major mood spoiler for your Hungarian Vizsla.

Brush its coat once or twice daily to keep the coat healthy. As far as its bath is concerned, build a monthly schedule that keeps your pet clean. If your puppy is not much of an inquisitive creature, you might delay its shower. See how your pet responds to the grooming needs in order to build a schedule that fits it perfectly.

Besides this, your Hungarian Vizsla needs to brush its teeth regularly in order to maintain its dental health. The same goes for ear care though the need to clean its ears becomes more pronounced once it has taken its periodic bath. Invest wisely in eye care as well. Keep in mind that the grooming efforts you make towards your pet define its health and wellness in the present as well as in the future.

It is easy to care for a Hungarian Vizsla dog. Apart from their amiable natures, their relatively low maintenance requirements are an added benefit. If you are planning to purchase a Hungarian Vizsla (or if you've already purchased one), rest assured it will be an amazing journey.

\Unless, of course, if you don't like being followed everywhere! That can be quite some problem with the Hungarian Vizsla breed!

Chapter 12: Training Your Hungarian Vizsla

Every dog needs to be trained. It is a way of introducing these creatures to the human life. It aims to discipline their behavior in a way that prevents them from creating mischief. Consequently, there would be fewer chances for it to be getting on your nerves. In essence, it ensures that your relationship with your pet is a pleasant one.

There are quite a few dog training courses available that you might be interested in. From specific training regimes to obedience training and others – there is a lot to be learned. Each dog training course comes with a cost. However, the benefits they offer often justify the investment you make.

If you are unsure about the courses you should pay for, you can always seek consultation and advice from the experts. Most of the dog training courses involve the role of a dog expert who can understand your pet and communicate with it in a seamless fashion. They are therefore in a better position to elaborate your dog's needs!

On this note, keep in mind that an apparently well-behaved dog is no guarantee for its training requirements. It takes a simple distraction to turn your pet against you. Especially during the mating season, it becomes exceptionally difficult to discipline the dog.

You need to put your dog through training courses – come what may! If you put it through the appropriate training courses early on, this will ensure a happy and healthy relationship through the rest of its life!

1) Your Pet Needs Training

With dogs, it is natural for them to seek a pecking order. It is like a hierarchy – who'll be the leader and who will be the follower. Anyone who isn't leading is inevitably following. Dogs in general like establishing their supremacy over their flock at the earliest possible.

This is one reason why it is stressed that dogs should be put to training during their early years. As soon as you bring the puppy home, the training begins. At that time, it is about disciplining the puppy to understand your supremacy. Later on, it is about training them to perform specific actions and avoid others.

An apparently well behaved Hungarian Vizsla does not guarantee the dog will behave the same way in face of distraction. Training ensures your dog responds to your call not just when it is in the mood to respond but also at times when it isn't. It gives you better control over its life and safety.

Imagine what'll happen if your puppy is devouring something that is dangerous and it refuses to respond to your orders? Adequate training ensures you can prevent costly accidents by ensuring your pet is responsive and disciplined.

2) Puppy Training Basics

First things first, it is important for you to decide which type of training method you are going to adopt. People usually go for the positive consequence reinforcement technique. This means that whenever the puppy acts according to your wishes, you'll grant it a treat in appreciation for its performance.

It makes perfect sense; reinforcing the positives periodically so that the puppy understands what is expected of it. Why is it then that people who use this technique in seclusion witness no quantitative results?

This method works fine when the puppy needs treats. If the puppy is feeling hungry or if it is simply greedy for treats, it will comply with your demands. But what happens when it is on a full stomach or whether it simply isn't interested to respond?

This is where the problem begins. You cannot expect the Hungarian Vizsla to respond in such situations. It will find the distraction much more attractive and will therefore not comply with your orders. In such situations, it wouldn't respond even if it puts itself in danger!

This is why it is important for you to impose a balanced form of training. While you should appreciate the rightly done chores through treats, you need to devise a method of penalizing it in case it fails to respond. The puppy will behave well not only because it feels like having treats but also because it wants to avoid the repercussions of not following the orders.

Make sure you have a very clear and direct expression to symbolize your unhappiness with your pet. The experts like referring to it as the "discipline sound". It can be anything ranging from a whistle or a simple "UH-OH" sound. Everyone should be consistent with the sound and the puppy should understand what it means; there will be little confusion in its mind about what is expected of it.

As long as there is a balance in the medium of training that you offer to the puppy, you'll be grooming it well. It will not only be a pleasant experience for you but also for your loved ones!

3) Acclimatization to the Leash

After bringing the puppy from the breeder's, you'll need to acclimatize it to the leash. It will be a new experience for your dog. Previously at the breeder's, the puppy is more likely to be a free entity. But when it moves in with you, it'll be an entirely different story.

Acclimatization with the leash is important for several reasons. Firstly, it helps you walk the puppy around the vicinity without worrying about it going haywire. The leash keeps you in control of the puppy's movements.

Moreover, the leash helps in disciplining the puppy while keeping it safe from all kinds of threats. In essence, leash training has a lot to offer; if only the puppy is introduced to it in the right manner.

Acclimatization with the leash takes time and effort. In the beginning, your puppy will most definitely resist it. This is a natural reaction on behalf of the puppy. However, through consistency and diligence, you will eventually be able to convince the puppy to follow your rules.

Fasten a dog collar and leash on your pet carefully. Make sure it is the right size or you might end up strangling it. Even if it resists the leash, put it on nevertheless. It will take some time but the outcome will definitely be a positive one.

Never pull the leash too hard or drag your puppy around with the leash. You need to hold it strongly without pulling at its neck and wait for a few moments. The puppy will eventually give in to your wishes and follow your steps. If it tries to resist again, repeat the same procedure. Being harsh with the puppy will only teach it to be rude and raucous.

On the same note, never allow the puppy to lead the way. When and if it tries to surpass you, hold the leash steadily, wait for a minute to let it come back to its position and then start over again. Every time it moves ahead of you, it begins to consider itself as the supreme one! You need to be careful about such behaviors in order to prevent long drawn troubles.

The puppy (especially the Hungarian Vizsla puppy) loves being around you and will definitely want to go out and about with you. On top of this, it has a naturally urge to roam around places. It will work out in your favor in the long run!

4) Walking

It is easily the best way to exercise your puppy every day. It comes in exceptionally handy for those who cannot afford going on weekly hikes or other similar activities. The least you can do to keep your pet from destroying your property is to take it out for a regular walk.

Never let it take the lead. And never take it out for a walk without the leash. You'd be inviting pure trouble if you are not following the basic rules. Besides these, never pull at the leash too hard. This piece of equipment is in place to discipline your pet and let it know when it is going out of bounds. You shouldn't use it to make your puppy walk forcefully. Just give it a moment to rethink its decision not to move; it will eventually understand what it is expected to be doing!

Let the Hungarian Vizsla follow you. If it tries to do otherwise, just give the leash a strong pull and wait for the puppy to decide. Use a good quality collar and leash to ensure the puppy's tender neck muscles do not get damaged. The rest should be fine!

5) Penalizing Unwanted Behaviors

Often owners make the mistake of accidentally rewarding unwanted behaviors.

It is very important to recognize that any attention paid to an overly excited, out of control, adolescent puppy – even negative attention – is more likely to be considered as rewarding for your puppy.

Therefore, when you engage with an out of control Hungarian Vizsla puppy, you end up actually rewarding them, which will encourage them to continue more of this unwanted behavior.

Be aware that chasing after a puppy when they have taken something they are not supposed to have, picking them up when they are barking or showing aggression, pushing them off when they jump on you or other people, or yelling when they refuse to come when called, are all forms of attention that can actually be rewarding for most puppies.

As your Hungarian Vizsla dog's guardian, it will be your responsibility to provide calm and consistent structure for your puppy, which will include finding acceptable and safe ways to allow your puppy to vent their energy without being destructive or harmful to property, other dogs, humans, or to itself.

Activities that create or encourage an overly excited Hungarian Vizsla puppy, such as rough games of tug-of-war, or wild games of chase through the living room, should be immediately curtailed, so that your adolescent puppy learns how to control their energy and play quietly and appropriately without jumping on everyone or engaging in barking or mouthy behavior.

Further, if an adolescent Hungarian Vizsla puppy displays excited energy simply from being petted by you, your family members or any visitors, you will need to teach yourself, your family and your friends to ignore your puppy until they calm down. Otherwise, you will be teaching your Hungarian Vizsla puppy that the touch of humans means excitement.

For instance, when you continue to engage with an overly excited puppy, you are rewarding them for out of control behavior and literally teaching them that when they see humans, you want them to display excited energy.

Worse, once your puppy has learned that humans are a source of excitement, you will then have to work very long and hard to reverse this behavior.

Children are often a source of excitement that can cause an adolescent puppy to be extremely wound up.

Do not allow your children to engage with an adolescent Hungarian Vizsla puppy unless you are there to supervise and teach the children appropriate and calm ways to interact with the puppy.

In order to keep everyone safe, it is very important that your Hungarian Vizsla puppy learns at an early age that neither children nor adults are sources of excitement.

You can help develop the mind of an adolescent Hungarian Vizsla and the minds of growing children at the same time by teaching children that your puppy needs structured walks and by showing them how to play fetch, search, hide and seek, or how to teach the Hungarian Vizsla puppy simple tricks and obedience skills that will be fun and positive interaction for everyone.

6) Maintaining Your Patience

What would you do if your Hungarian Vizsla dog still fails to perform the way you want it to?

Whatever you do, don't shout, holler or physically hurt it. Your Hungarian Vizsla dog is not a puppet that will follow your orders perfectly every time.

Making mistakes every now and then is perfectly normal for this animal. It will take time and patience to train your Hungarian Vizsla dog and have it follow your wishes. It does not happen overnight.

So if you are under the impression that training sessions begin yielding results right away, clear the misconception before penalizing your pet.

In any case, if you are penalizing your pet too often on things of no or negligible value, you will end up scarring its personality. The Hungarian Vizsla dog will become disturbed and develop more behavioral issues.

Before getting your pet home, learn to be patient with those that are not subservient to you. Once you've learnt this valuable trait, only then proceed with your Hungarian Vizsla purchase.

Your pet is not something you can abuse simply because you had a bad time at the office; it is a living being just like you. Care and respect it - that is all that it needs!

7) Consistency and Perseverance

When you enroll your Hungarian Vizsla in any of the training lessons, make sure you take it in for the session for the entire duration of the course. Just because your pet apparently seems to be behaving well shouldn't encourage you not to take your pet for further sessions.

For the training sessions to be truly effective and long-lasting, it is important for you to remain consistent with the lessons. For all you know, by missing out on any session, you might be reinforcing negative traits in the Hungarian Vizsla dog.

Take your pet in for the training lessons regularly. It is best if the lessons are done with during its early years. This helps integrate the lessons and values into the pet's behavior which in turn yields lasting results.

On the same note, it is better if you don't leave your Hungarian Vizsla on someone else to take it to the training courses. As the owner and as the leader, it is important for you to be personally present at all the training sessions to reinforce your authority.

Beware of those dog training centers which offer to take your pet in and deliver back a well disciplined dog. No one can teach the dog to respect you other than yourself. The canine naturally gives respect to those who it considers as the leader. Without your active participation, no one can inculcate that thought.

That being said; be regular with your puppy's appointments – whether it is the trip to the veterinary doctor or to the trainer. Consistency and perseverance wins the race!

8) Using Hand Signals and Speech

Make sure you put your pet through the speech training first. Use consistent words to tell the puppy what needs to be done. Three of the most basic orders you'd want the puppy to follow are "Come", "Sit" and "Stay". The treat method will be quite effective in training the puppy to follow these orders.

Make sure you are using the same words for the same actions. If you try to discipline the puppy with different words, it will become confused about what is being expected of it. Consequently, it will be unable to respond productively.

Always conduct speech training before moving on with hand signals. This ensures your pet will be able to follow the hand signals properly when you proceed forward.

Hand signal training is by far the most useful and efficient training method for every dog, including the Hungarian Vizsla. This is because all too often we inundate our canine companions with a great deal of chatter and noise that they really do not understand because English is not their first language.

Contrary to what some humans might think, the first language of a Hungarian Vizsla, or any dog, is a combination of sensing energy and watching body language, which requires no spoken word or sound. In fact, the puppy learns to respond to the sounds by observing the energies and body language!

Therefore, when we humans take the time to teach our dog hand signals for all their basic commands, we are communicating with them at a level they instinctively understand, plus we are helping them to become a focused follower, as they must watch us to understand what is required of them.

Come: you can kneel down for this command or stay standing. Open your arms wide like you are hugging a very large tree. This hand signal should be seen from a long distance.

When first teaching hand signals to your Hungarian Vizsla, always show the hand signal for the command at the same time you say the word.

If they are totally ignoring the command, it will be time to incorporate a lunge line, which is a very long leash to help you teach the "Come" command.

Simply attach a 20-foot line to their collar and let them sniff about in a large yard or at your neighborhood park.

At your leisure, firmly ask them to "Come" and show the hand signal. If they do not immediately come to you, give a firm tug with the lunge line, so that they understand what you are asking of them.

If they still do not "Come" toward you, simply reel them in until they are in front of you. Then let them wander about again, until you are ready to ask them to "Come".

Repeat this process until your Hungarian Vizsla responds correctly at least 80% of the time. You can also reinforce the command by giving a treat when they come back to you when asked. Always ask them to "Sit" when they come to you.

Sit: right arm (palm open facing upward) parallel to the floor, and then raise your arm, while bent at the elbow toward your shoulder.

Sit is a very simple, yet extremely valuable command for all puppies and dogs.

If your dog is not sitting on command, try holding a treat above and slightly behind their head, so that when they look up for it they may automatically sit to see it.

Slowly remove the treats as reward and replace the treat with a "live reward", such as a chest rub or a scratch behind the ears and your happy smile.

If your Hungarian Vizsla is not particularly treat motivated, lift up and slightly back on the leash when asking them to sit (stand in front of them), and if they still are having difficulties, reach down with your free hand, place it across your dog's back at the place where the back legs join the hip and gently squeeze.

Remember -- Do NOT simply push down on your dog's back to force their hind legs to collapse under them as this pressure could harm their spine or leg joints.

Stay: right arm fully extended toward your dog's head, palm open, hand bent up at the wrist.

Once your Hungarian Vizsla is in the "Sit" position, ask them to "Stay" with both the verbal cue and the hand signal.

TIP: if you are right-handed, use your right arm and hand for the signal, and if you are left-handed, use your left arm and hand for the signal. Using your dominant hand will be much more effective because the strongest energy emanates from the palm of your dominant hand.

While your dog is sitting and staying, slowly back away from them. If they move from their position, calmly put them back into Sit and ask them to "Stay" again, using both the verbal cue and the hand signal.

Continue to practice this until your dog understands that you want them to stay sitting and not move toward you.

With all commands, when your Hungarian Vizsla is just learning, be patient and always reward them with a treat and your happy praise for a job well done.

9) *Adult Training*

By the time your puppy approaches the age of six months to one year, it will be appropriate to consider it as an adult. It will resemble a fully matured Hungarian Vizsla. Moreover, it will begin taking its own decisions. It is primarily a learning stage for your Hungarian Vizsla but it can be pretty tough on you as well as on your puppy.

It takes time to build a relationship of trust and respect with your puppy. But this is a phase in which your puppy will exhibit quite a few qualities that might get on your nerves. The Hungarian Vizsla may choose to selectively ignore your commands, destroy property that it did not find particularly interesting previously and also explore boundaries which it did not want to surpass previously.

Much of this can be attributed to the natural aging process. Some part of it can be attributed with their hormonal changes. This is also the time when your puppy will first experience the heat cycle. Since the feeling is new to it, you can expect all sorts of weird reactions to it.

This reinforces the thought; it takes consistency and perseverance in training to yield a well disciplined puppy. Just because you've taken your companion to training sessions as a puppy does not mean it will behave well during adulthood.

In fact, apparently well-behaved dogs are the first sign of trouble. Unless you continue with the advanced dog training sessions, your canine companion will definitely go haywire. It will test your patience to the extent that you might start reconsidering your decision to take in a canine companion.

It takes patience and perseverance to land in a well-rounded relationship with the dog. Make sure you don't skip out on its training sessions. Also, use the right kind of preventive measures to withhold its behavior.

For instance, spaying or neutering the puppy can put an end to its sexual agitation. Although this doesn't really imply a full stop to the process, it does relieve the major symptoms.

You need to support your companion through adulthood in the same way as you've supported it through puppyhood. On its own, the puppy is a threat to itself! And without your leadership and guidance, it is more likely to go astray! Fulfill the responsibilities you've taken on yourself through the acquisition process. The rest should be fine!

10) Handling Behavioral Issues

If your dog misbehaves once or twice, it can be fixed with proper training. But if the problems persist, it is a sure sign of behavioral issues.

On the whole, it is impossible to generalize what could or could not cause behavioral issues in pets. It depends on the individual situations, specimens, humans and all other things involved.

Just because the neighbor's dog had a particular problem does not justify your pet having the same. You cannot assess your pet on the basis of some text you read out of a particular book. Behavioral issues require in-depth personalized studies to identify a particular problem with a case.

You might need to hire the services of a dog whisperer or a dog psychologist for this cause. The expert will be in a better state to understand the problems by asking specific questions and analyzing the situation.

Be honest with the dog expert when you are required to answer a few questions – this will help you get to the bottom of it with ease.

The key to resolving behavioral issues lies in understanding the problems in the first place.

11) House Training or House "Breaking"

House training, house breaking, or *"potty"* training, is a critical first step in the education of any new puppy, and the first part of a successful process is training the human guardian.

When you bring home your new Hungarian Vizsla puppy, they will be relying upon your guidance to teach them what they need to learn.

When you provide your puppy with your consistent patience and understanding, they are capable of learning rules at a very early age, and house training is no different, especially since it's all about establishing a regular routine.

Potty training a new puppy takes time and patience — how much time depends entirely upon you.

Check in with yourself and make sure your energy remains consistently calm and patient and that you exercise plenty of compassion and understanding while you help your new puppy learn their new bathroom rules.

Hungarian Vizsla puppies and dogs flourish with routines and happily, so do humans, therefore, the first step is to establish a daily routine that will work well for both canine and human alike.

For instance, depending upon the age of your Hungarian Vizsla puppy, make a plan to take them out for a bathroom break every two hours and stick to it because while you are in the beginning stages of potty training, the more vigilant and consistent you can be the quicker and more successful your results will be.

Generally speaking, while your puppy is still growing, a young puppy can hold it approximately one hour for every month of their age.

This means that if your 2-month-old puppy has been happily snoozing for a couple of hours, as soon as they wake up, they will need to go outside.

Some of the first indications or signs that your puppy needs to be taken outside to relieve themselves will be when you see them:

- sniffing around
- circling
- looking for the door
- whining, crying or barking
- acting agitated

It will be important to always take your Hungarian Vizsla puppy out first thing every morning, and immediately after they wake up from a nap as well as soon after they have finished eating a meal or having a big drink of water.

Also, your happy praise goes a long way toward encouraging and reinforcing future success when your Hungarian Vizsla puppy makes the right decisions, so let them know you are happy when they do their business in the right place.

Initially, treats can be a good way to reinforce how pleased you are that your puppy is learning to go potty in the right place. Slowly treats can be removed and replaced with your happy praise.

Next, now that you have a new puppy in your life, you will want to be flexible with respect to adapting your schedule. You need to accommodate the requirements of your Hungarian Vizsla puppy that will get it accustomed to their new bathroom routine.

This means not leaving your puppy alone for endless hours at a time because firstly, they are sensitive pack animals that need companionship and your direction at all times, plus long periods alone will result in the disruption of the potty training schedule you have worked hard to establish.

If you have no choice but to leave your puppy alone for many hours, make sure that you place them in a paper lined room or pen where they can relieve themselves without destroying your favorite carpet or new hardwood flooring.

Remember, your Hungarian Vizsla is a growing puppy with a bladder and bowels that they do not yet have complete control over. You will have a much happier time and better success if you simply train yourself to pay attention. Know when the young companion is showing signs of needing to relieve themselves – it'll be the beginning of a promising tomorrow.

12) Bell Training

A very easy way to introduce your new Hungarian Vizsla puppy to house training is to begin by teaching them how to ring a doorbell whenever they need to go outside.

Ringing a doorbell is not only a convenient alert system for both you and your Hungarian Vizsla puppy or dog, your visitors will be most impressed by how smart your Hungarian Vizsla is.

A further benefit of training your puppy to ring a bell is that you will not have to listen to your puppy/dog whining, barking or howling to be let out and your door will not be scratched from its nails.

Unless you prefer to purchase an already manufactured doggy doorbell or system, take a trip to your local novelty store and purchase a small bell that has a nice, loud ring.

Attach the bell to a piece of ribbon or string and hang it from a door handle or tape it to a door sill near the door where you will be taking your puppy out when they need to relieve themselves. The string will need to be long enough so that your Hungarian Vizsla puppy can easily reach the bell with their nose or a paw.

Next, each time you take your puppy out to go potty, say the word *"Out"*, and use their paw or their nose to ring the bell. Praise them for this *"trick"* and immediately take them outside.

The only down side to teaching your Hungarian Vizsla puppy or dog to ring a bell when they want to go outside, is that even if they don't actually have to go out to relieve themselves, but just want to go outside because they are bored, you will still have to take them out every time they ring the bell.

There are many types and styles of *"gotta' go"* commercially manufactured bells you could choose, ranging from the elegant **"Poochie Bells™"** that hang from a doorknob, the simple **"Tell Bell™"** that sits on the floor, or various high tech door chime systems that function much like a doggy intercom system where they push a pad with their paw and it rings a bell.

Whatever doorbell system you choose for your Hungarian Vizsla puppy, once they are trained, this type of an alert system is an easy way to eliminate accidents in the home.

13) Free Training

Free training is when you allow the puppy to roam around the house without restrictions. They are not confined to a room or two – they are trained to move around the house without causing accidents.

For the most part, the Velcro nature of Hungarian Vizslas makes it impossible for you to keep it locked away in kennels or puppy apartments. It will simply not respond to it as you would want it to. In fact, you will end up creating problems for yourself if you try to keep it locked away in confinements. The Hungarian Vizsla tends to become extremely rebellious if it is confined.

The Hungarian Vizsla craves the human touch. Free training is the only viable course of action you can employ with this breed.

Keep in mind that it requires extensive supervision in order to train the puppy to move freely. You'll need to be on your watch at all times to understand when it is experiencing the call of nature. There may be a few accidents every now and then. You need to be patient with your pet.

Avoid hollering at your pet or getting upset with it. It does not understand what is wrong with relieving itself. Whenever you catch the pet in the act at the wrong place, just say it is wrong. Say strongly, "NO!" and pick it up to take it to the spot. It will eventually understand what is expected of it and where it is going wrong.

Alternatively, puppy pee pads will be a good idea to prevent initial accidents. However, you cannot use these in the long run. You'll need to bear with a few accidents in order to teach your pet a lasting lesson.

You need to be absolutely patient and compassionate with your pet during this period. The moment you get agitated, the puppy will become worried. This, in turn, may lead to medical and behavioral problems. Rest assured, when it is done, you'll be glad to have undertaken the time and pain to teach your pet this valuable lesson.

14) Electronic Devices Training

In general, electronic devices training is not recommended for any dog breed. The use of e-collars, spray collars and invisible electrical fences make use of negative consequence in order inhibit an activity. The truth is, if your pet doesn't know where or how it is going wrong, it is least likely to understand why it is being penalized.

The use of electronic training devices is a pretty controversial topic in itself. For smaller breeds, they are an absolute must-avoid. For the larger ones, it can be used to control extremely dangerous reactions. For instance, if your dog is about to hurt someone or itself, the electronic training devices may come in handy.

For the Hungarian Vizsla in particular, the use of electronic training devices is not recommended. They would be more than willing to take orders directly from you and following them precisely rather than being electrocuted. If you train your puppy and dog well, you wouldn't need to rely on such extreme techniques to tame your pet!

For the most part, the Hungarian Vizsla responds well to positive consequence reinforcements. You don't need to go these lengths to inhibit its mischief. But if you do, make sure you don't use it often. You might end up doing some serious damage to your pet.

15) Simple Tips and Tricks for Training

When teaching your Hungarian Vizsla tricks, in order to give them extra incentive, find a treat that they really like, and give the treat as a reward to help solidify a good performance. Most dogs will be extra attentive during training sessions when they know that they will be rewarded with their favorite treats.

If your Hungarian Vizsla is less than six months old when you begin teaching them tricks, keep your training sessions short (no more than 5 or 10 minutes) and fun, and as they become adults, you can extend your sessions as they will be able to maintain their focus for longer periods of time.

Shake a Paw

Who doesn't love a dog that knows how to shake a paw? This is one of the easiest tricks to teach your Hungarian Vizsla.

Most dogs are naturally either right or left pawed. If you know which paw your dog favors, ask them to shake this paw.

Find a quiet place to practice, without noisy distractions or other pets, and stand or sit in front of your dog. Place them in the sitting position and have a treat in your left hand.

Say the command *"Shake"* while putting your right hand behind their left or right paw and pulling the paw gently toward yourself until you are holding their paw in your hand. Immediately praise them and give them the treat.

Most dogs will learn the "Shake" trick very quickly, and very soon, once you put out your hand, your Hungarian Vizsla will immediately lift their paw and put it into your hand, without your assistance or any verbal cue.

Practice every day until they are 100% reliable with this trick, and then it will be time to add another trick to their repertoire.

Roll Over

You will find that just like your Hungarian Vizsla is naturally either right or left pawed, that they will also naturally want to roll either to the right or the left side. Take advantage of this by asking your dog to roll to the side they naturally prefer.

Sit with your dog on the floor and put them in a lie down position. Hold a treat in your hand and place it close to their nose without allowing them to grab it, and while they are in the lying position, move the treat to the right or left side of their head so that they have to roll over to get to it.

You will very quickly see which side they want to naturally roll to, and once you see this, move the treat to this side. Once they roll over to this side, immediately give them the treat and praise them.

You can say the verbal cue *"Over"* while you demonstrate the hand signal motion (moving your right hand in a circular motion) or moving the treat from one side of their head to the other with a half circle motion.

Once your Hungarian Vizsla can roll over every time you ask, it will be time to teach them another trick.

Sit Pretty

While this trick is a little more complicated, and most dogs pick up on it very quickly, remember that every dog is different so always exercise patience.

Find a quiet space with few distractions and sit or stand in front of your dog and ask them to "Sit".

Have a treat nearby (on a countertop or table) and when they sit, use both of your hands to lift up their front paws into the sitting pretty position, while saying the command *"Sit Pretty"*. Help them balance in this position while you praise them and give them the treat.

Once your Hungarian Vizsla can do the balancing part of the trick quite easily without your help, sit or stand in front of your dog while asking them to *"Sit Pretty"* and hold the treat above their head, at the level their nose would be when they sit pretty.

When first beginning this trick, place your Hungarian Vizsla beside a wall so they can use the wall to help them balance. If they attempt to stand on their back legs to get the treat, you may be holding the treat too high, which will encourage them to stand on their back legs to reach it. Go back to the first step and put them back into the *"Sit"* position and again lift their paws while their backside remains on the floor.

Hold your straight arm, fully extended, over your dog's head with a closed fist. Make this a fun and entertaining time for your Hungarian Vizsla and practice a few times every day until they can *"Sit Pretty"* on hand signal command every time you ask.

A young Hungarian Vizsla puppy should be able to easily learn these basic tricks before they are six months old and when you are patient and make your training sessions short and fun for your dog, they will be eager to learn more.

16) Handling Accidents While Training

Remember that a dog's sense of smell is at least 2,000 times more sensitive that our human sense of smell.

As a result of your Hungarian Vizsla puppy's superior sense of smell, it will be very important to effectively remove all odors from house training accidents; otherwise, your Hungarian Vizsla puppy will be attracted by the smell to the place where they may have had a previous accident, and will want to do their business there again and again.

While there are many products that are supposed to remove odors and stains, many of these are not very effective. You want a professional grade cleaner that will not just mask one odor with another scent; you want a product that will completely neutralize odors.

Go to RemoveUrineOdors.com and order yourself some *"SUN"* and/or *"Max Enzyme"* because these products contain professional-strength odor neutralizers and urine digesters that bind to and completely absorb odors on any type of surface.

Chapter 13: Medical Concerns

The Hungarian Vizsla is generally a sprightly dog that loves being around people. On the whole, the breed is considered to be a healthy one. But there are quite a few health concerns you need to be worried about while bringing the Hungarian Vizsla home.

The key to a healthy and happy relationship with your pet lies in caring for your pet's needs. One of the most crucial needs include being mindful of its health. The Hungarian Vizsla is prone to a number of health problems.

While there isn't much you can do if your canine companion is destined to fall ill, there is a lot you can do to diagnose the problem as early as possible. This way, you can save your pet from a lot of unnecessary pain and trouble.

Here's how you can keep a watch on your pet's health concerns. It is one of your prime-most responsibilities. Make sure you've built a contingency for it already before you bring your puppy in.

1) Tips for Choosing a Veterinarian

A consideration to keep in mind when choosing a veterinarian clinic will be that some clinics specialize in caring for smaller pets, and some specialize in caring for the large sized animals, while still others have a wide ranging area of expertise and will care for all animals, including livestock and reptiles.

Choosing a clinic will be a personal decision, however, since the Hungarian Vizsla is considered as a medium sized breed, your dog's needs may be better served by choosing a clinic that specializes in the care of small to medium sized pets.

Choosing a good veterinary clinic will be very similar to choosing the right health care clinic or doctor for your own personal health because you want to ensure that your Hungarian Vizsla puppy receives the quality care they deserve.

Begin your search by asking other dog owners where they take their furry and hairy friends and whether they are happy with the service they receive.

If you don't know anyone to ask, visit the local pet store in your area as they should be able to provide you with references and local listings of pet care clinics.

Next, check online, because a good pet clinic will have an active website up and running that will list details of all the services they provide along with an overview of all staff members, their education and qualifications.

Once you've narrowed your search, it's time to personally visit the clinics you may be interested in, as this will be a good opportunity for you to visually inspect the facility, interact with the staff and perhaps meet the veterinarians face to face.

Of course, it's not just you who needs to feel comfortable with the clinic chosen and those working there. Your puppy needs to feel comfortable, too, and this is where visiting a clinic and interacting with the staff and veterinarians will provide you with an idea of their experience and expertise in handling your puppy.

If your puppy is comfortable with them, then you will be much more likely to trust that they will be providing the best care for your puppy that will need to receive all their vaccinations and yearly check-ups, and eventually be spayed or neutered.

It's also a good idea to take your puppy into your chosen clinic several times before they actually need to be there for any treatment, so that they are not fearful of the new smells and unfamiliar surroundings.

2) Neutering and Spaying

It can sometimes be difficult to find a definitive answer for the question what is the best time to neuter or spay your young Hungarian Vizsla. The topic itself is pretty controversial among dog enthusiasts. There are a number of varying opinions on this topic. One thing that most veterinarians do agree on is that earlier spaying or neutering, between 4 and 6 months of age, is a better choice than waiting.

Spaying or neutering surgeries are carried out under general anesthesia. These days, more dogs are being neutered at younger ages. Make sure you speak with your veterinarian and ask for their recommendations regarding the right age to spay or neuter your Hungarian Vizsla.

Effects on Aggression

Intact (non-neutered) males and females are more likely to display aggression related to sexual behavior than are dogs that have been neutered or spayed.

Fighting, particularly in male dogs that are directed at other males, is less common after neutering, and the intensity of other types of aggression, such as irritable aggression in females will be totally eliminated by spaying.

While neutering or spaying is not a treatment for aggression, it can certainly help to minimize the severity and escalation of aggressiveness and is often the first step toward resolving an aggressive behavior problem.

What is Neutering?

Neutering is a surgical procedure, carried out by a licensed veterinarian surgeon to render a male dog unable to reproduce.

In males, the surgery is also referred to as *"castration"* because the procedure entails the removal of the young dog's testicles. When the testicles are removed, what is left behind is an empty scrotal sac (which used to contain the puppy's testicles) and this empty sac will soon shrink in size until it is no longer noticeable.

Neutering Males

Neutering male Hungarian Vizsla puppies before they are six months of age can help to ensure that they will be less likely to suffer from obesity problems when they grow older.

Neutering can also mean that a male Hungarian Vizsla will be less likely to have the urge to wander.

Further, waiting until a male Hungarian Vizsla is older than six months before having them neutered could mean that they will experience the effects of raging testosterone that will drive them to escape their yards by any means necessary to search out females to mate with.

Non-neutered males also tend to spray or mark territory much more often, both inside and outside the home, and during this time can start to display aggressive tendencies toward other dogs as well as people.

What is Spaying?

In female puppies, sterilization, referred to as *"spaying"*, is a surgical procedure carried out by a licensed veterinarian, to prevent the female dog from becoming pregnant and to stop regular heat cycles.

The sterilization procedure is much more involved for a female puppy (than for a male), as it requires the removal of both ovaries and the uterus by incision into the puppy's abdominal cavity. The uterus is also removed during this surgery, to prevent the possibility of it becoming infected later on in life.

Spaying Females

Preferably, female Hungarian Vizsla puppies should be spayed before their very first estrus or heat cycle. Females in heat often appear more agitated and irritable, while sleeping and eating less and some may become extremely aggressive toward other dogs.

Spaying female puppies before their first heat pattern can eliminate these hormonal stressors and reduce the opportunity of mammary glandular tumors. Early spaying also protects against various other potential concerns, such as uterine infections.

Effects on General Temperament

Many dog owners often become needlessly worried that a neutered or spayed dog will lose their vigor. Rest assured that a dog's personality or energy level will not be modified or altered in any way by the neutering process. In fact, many unfavorable qualities resulting from hormonal impact may resolve after surgery.

Your Hungarian Vizsla will certainly not come to be less caring or cheerful, and neither will he or she resent you because you are not denying your dog any essential encounters. You will, however, be acting as a conscientious, informed, and caring Hungarian Vizsla guardian.

Further, there is little evidence to suggest that the nature of a female Hungarian Vizsla will improve after having a litter of puppies. What is important is that you do not project your own psychological needs or concerns onto your Hungarian Vizsla puppy, because there is no gain to be had from permitting sexual activity in either male or female canines.

For instance, it is not *"abnormal"* or *"mean"* to manage a puppy's reproductive activity by having them sterilized. Rather, it is unkind and irresponsible not to neuter or spay a dog and there are many positive benefits of having this procedure carried out.

Effects on Escape and Roaming

A neutered or spayed Hungarian Vizsla is less likely to wander. Castrated male dogs have the tendency to patrol smaller sized outdoor areas and are less likely to participate in territorial conflicts with perceived opponents.

A Hungarian Vizsla that has actually already experienced successful escapes from the yard may continue to wander after they are spayed or neutered.

Effects on Problem Elimination

An unsterilized dog may urinate or defecate inside the home or in other undesirable areas in an attempt to stake territorial claims, relieve anxiety, or advertise their available reproductive status.

Neutering or spaying a Hungarian Vizsla puppy after they have already begun to inappropriately eliminate or mark territory to announce their sexual availability to other dogs will reduce the more powerful urine odor as well as eliminate the hormonal factors. However, once this habit has begun, the undesirable behavior may continue to persist even after neutering or spaying.

Possible Weight Gain

While metabolic changes that occur after spaying or neutering can cause some Hungarian Vizsla puppy's to gain weight, often the real culprit for any weight gain is the human. It is normal for you to feel guilty for subjecting your puppy to the pain of sterilization. However, it doesn't justify feeding more treats or meals to your Hungarian Vizsla companion in order to make up.

If you are concerned about weight gain after neutering or spaying a Hungarian Vizsla puppy, simply adjust their food and treat consumption, as needed, and make sure that they receive adequate daily exercise.

It's a very simply process to change your Hungarian Vizsla dog's food intake according to their physical demands and how they look, and if your Hungarian Vizsla puppy's daily exercise and level of activity has not changed after they have been spayed or neutered, there will likely be no change in food management necessary.

3) Vaccinations

Puppies need to be vaccinated by a veterinarian in order to provide them with protection against four common and serious diseases.

Vaccination against this common set of diseases is referred to as ***"DAPP"***, which stands for **D**istemper, **A**denovirus, **P**arainfluenza and **P**arvo Virus.

Approximately one week after your Hungarian Vizsla puppy has completed all three sets of primary DAPP vaccinations they will be fully protected from those specific diseases. Thereafter, most veterinarians will recommend a once a year vaccination for the next year or two.

It has now become common practice to vaccinate adult dogs every three years, and if your veterinarian is insisting on a yearly vaccination for your Hungarian Vizsla puppy, you need to ask them why, because to do otherwise is considered by most professionals to be *"over vaccinating"*.

Distemper

Canine distemper is a contagious and serious viral illness for which there is currently no known cure.

This deadly virus, which is spread either through the air or by direct or indirect contact with a dog that is already infected or other distemper-carrying wildlife, including ferrets, raccoons, foxes, skunks and wolves, is a relative of the measles virus which affects humans.

Canine distemper is sometimes also called *"hard pad disease"* because some strains of the distemper virus actually cause thickening of the pads on a dog's feet, which can also affect the end of a dog's nose.

In dogs or animals with weak immune systems, death may result two to five weeks after the initial distemper infection.

Early symptoms of distemper include fever, loss of appetite, and mild eye inflammation that may only last a day or two. Symptoms become more serious and noticeable as the disease progresses.

A puppy or dog that survives the distemper virus will usually continue to experience symptoms or signs of the disease throughout their remaining lifespan, including *"hard pad disease"* as well as *"enamel hypoplasia"*, which is damage to the enamel of the puppy's teeth that are not yet formed or that have not yet pushed through the gums.

Enamel hypoplasia is caused when the distemper virus kills the cells that manufacture tooth enamel.

Adenovirus

It is a virus that causes infectious canine hepatitis, which can range in severity from very mild to very serious, sometimes resulting in death.

Symptoms can include coughing, loss of appetite, increased thirst and urination, tiredness, runny eyes and nose, vomiting, bruising or bleeding under the skin, swelling of the head, neck and body, fluid accumulation in the abdomen area, jaundice (yellow tinge to the skin), a bluish clouding of the cornea of the eye (called "hepatitis blue eye") and seizures.

There is no specific treatment for infectious canine hepatitis. Treatment of the disease is focused on managing symptoms while the virus runs its course. Hospitalization and intravenous fluid therapy may be required in severe cases.

Canine Parainfluenza Virus

The canine parainfluenza virus (CPIV) also referred to as *"canine influenza virus"*, *"greyhound disease"* or *"race flu"*, which is easily spread through the air or by coming into contact with respiratory secretions, was originally a virus that only affected horses.

This disease is believed to have adapted to become contagious to dogs, is easily spread from dog to dog, and may cause symptoms that become fatal.

While the more frequent occurrences of this respiratory infection are seen in areas where there are high dog populations, such as race tracks, boarding kennels and pet stores, this virus is highly contagious to any dog or puppy, at any age.

Symptoms can include a dry, hacking cough, difficulty breathing, wheezing, runny nose and eyes, sneezing, fever, loss of appetite, tiredness, depression and possible pneumonia.

In cases where only a cough exists, tests will be required to determine whether the cause of the cough is the parainfluenza virus or the less serious *"kennel cough"*.

While many dogs can naturally recover from this virus, they will remain contagious, and for this reason, in order to prevent the spread to other animals, aggressive treatment of the virus, with antibiotics and antiviral drugs will be the general course of action.

In more severe cases, a cough suppressant may be prescribed, as well as intravenous fluids to help prevent secondary bacterial infection.

Canine Parvovirus

Canine parvovirus (CPV) is a highly contagious viral illness affecting puppies and dogs. Parvovirus also affects other canine species including foxes, coyotes and wolves.

There are two forms of this virus (1) the more common intestinal form, and (2) the less common cardiac form, which can cause death in young puppies.

Symptoms of the intestinal form of parvovirus include vomiting, bloody diarrhea, weight loss, and lack of appetite, while the less common cardiac form attacks the heart muscle.

Early vaccination in young puppies has radically reduced the incidence of canine parvovirus infection, which is easily transmitted either by direct contact with an infected dog, or indirectly, by sniffing an infected dog's feces.

The virus can also be brought into a dog's environment on the bottom of human shoes that may have stepped on infected feces, and there is evidence that this hardy virus can live in ground soil for up to a year.

Recovery from parvovirus requires both aggressive and early treatment. With proper treatment, death rates are relatively low (between 5 and 20%), although chances of survival for puppies are much lower than for older dogs, and in all instances, there is no guarantee of survival.

Treatment of parvovirus requires hospitalization where intravenous fluids and nutrients are administered to help combat dehydration. As well, antibiotics will be given to counteract secondary bacterial infections, and as necessary, medications to control nausea and vomiting may also be given.

Without prompt and proper treatment, dogs that have severe parvovirus infections can die within 48 to 72 hours.

4) Diseases and Viruses to Look Out For

There are several diseases out there that you need to be careful about. Here are a few common diseases and viruses that you should be looking out for. Consult a veterinary doctor immediately if anything about your pet doesn't seem to be right! Also, ask your veterinary doctor to suggest any additional vaccinations if possible!

a) Rabies

Rabies is a viral disease transmitted by coming into contact with the saliva of an infected animal, usually through a bite.

The virus travels to the brain along the nerves and once symptoms develop, death is almost certainly inevitable, usually following a prolonged period of suffering.

If you plan to travel out of State or across country borders, you will need to make sure that your Hungarian Vizsla has an up to date Rabies Vaccination Certificate (NASPHV form 51) indicating they have been inoculated against rabies.

Vaccinating dogs against rabies is also compulsory in most countries in mainland Europe, as is permanent identification and registration of dogs through the use of a Pet Passport.

Those living in a country that is rabies free (UK, Eire) are not required to vaccinate their dogs against rabies, unless they intend to travel.

b) Leishmaniasis

Leishmaniasis is caused by a parasite and is transmitted by a bite from a sand fly.

There is no definitive answer for effectively combating Leishmaniasis, especially since one vaccine will not prevent the known multiple species.

In areas where the known cause is a sand fly, deltamethrin collars (containing a neurotoxic insecticide) worn by the dogs has been proven to be 86% effective.

There are two types of Leishmaniasis: (1) a skin reaction causing hair loss, lesions and ulcerative dermatitis, and (2) a more severe, abdominal organ reaction, which is also known as *"black fever"*. When the disease affects organs of the abdominal cavity the symptoms include:

- loss of appetite
- diarrhea
- severe weight loss
- exercise intolerance
- vomiting
- nose bleed
- tarry feces
- fever
- pain in the joints
- excessive thirst and urination
- inflammation of the muscles

Leishmaniasis spreads throughout the body to most organs, with kidney failure being the most common cause of death. Virtually all infected dogs develop this system wide disease and as much as 90% of those infected will also display skin reactions.

Affected dogs in the US are frequently found to have acquired this infection in another country.

It is important to note that this disease is regularly found in the Middle East, the area around the Mediterranean basin, Portugal, Spain, Africa, South and Central America, southern Mexico and the US, with regular cases reported in Oklahoma and Ohio, where it is found in 20 to 40% of the dog population.

There have also been a few reported cases in Switzerland, northern France and the Netherlands.

Leishmaniasis is a *"zoonotic"* infection, which is a contagious disease that can be spread between both animals and humans.

This means that the organisms residing in the Leishmaniasis lesions can be communicated to humans.

Treatment in dogs is often difficult and the dog may suffer from relapses. Leishmaniasis poses a significant risk to the health of your dog, especially if you travel to the Mediterranean.

c) Lyme Disease

This is one of the most common tick-borne diseases in the world, which is transmitted by Borrelia bacteria found in the deer or sheep tick.

Lyme disease, also called *"borreliosis"*, is also a zoonotic disease that can affect both humans and dogs and this disease can be fatal.

The Borrelia bacteria that causes Lyme's disease, is transmitted by slow-feeding, hard-shelled deer or sheep ticks, and the tick usually has to be attached to the dog for a minimum of 18 hours before the infection is transmitted.

Symptoms of this disease in a young or adult dog include:

- recurrent lameness from joint inflammation
- lack of appetite
- depression
- stiff walk with arched back
- sensitivity to touch
- swollen lymph nodes

- fever
- kidney damage
- rare heart or nervous system complications

While Lyme disease has been reported in dogs throughout the United States and Europe, it is most prevalent in the upper Mid-Western states, the Atlantic seaboard, and the Pacific coastal states.

In order to properly diagnose and treat Lyme disease, blood tests will be required, and if the tests are positive, oral antibiotics will be prescribed to treat the conditions.

Prevention is the key to keeping this disease under control because dogs that have had Lyme disease before are still able to get the disease again.

There is a vaccine for Lyme disease and dogs living in areas that have easy access to these ticks should be vaccinated yearly.

d) Rocky Mountain Spotted Fever

This tick-transmitted disease is very often seen in dogs in the East, Midwest, and plains region of the US. The organisms causing Rocky Mountain Spotted Fever (RMSF) are transmitted by both the American dog tick and the RMSF tick, which must be attached to the dog for a minimum of five hours in order to transmit the disease.

Common symptoms of RMSF include:

- fever
- reduced appetite
- depression
- pain in the joints
- lameness
- vomiting
- diarrhea

Some dogs affected with RMSF may develop heart abnormalities, pneumonia, kidney failure, liver damage, or even neurological signs, such as seizures or unsteady, wobbly or stumbling gait.

Diagnosis of this disease requires blood testing and if the results are positive, oral antibiotics will be given to the infected dog for approximately two weeks.

Dogs that can clear the organism from their systems will recover and after being infected, will remain immune to future infection.

e) Ehrlichiosis

This is another tick borne disease transmitted by both the brown dog tick and the Lone Star Tick.

Ehrlichiosis has been reported in every state in the US, as well as worldwide. Common symptoms include:

- depression
- reduced appetite
- fever
- stiff and painful joints
- bruising

Signs of infection typically occur less than a month after a tick bite and last for approximately four weeks. There is no vaccine available.

Blood tests may be required to test for antibodies and treatment will require a course of antibiotics for up to four weeks in order to completely clear the organism from the infected dog's system.

After a dog has been previously infected, they may develop antibodies to the organism, but will not be immune to being re-infected.

Dogs living in areas of the country where the Ehrlichiosis tick diseases are common or widespread may be prescribed low doses of antibiotics during tick season.

f) Anaplasmosis

Deer ticks and western blacklegged ticks are carriers of the bacteria that transmit canine Anaplasmosis.

However, there is also another form of Anaplasmosis (caused by different bacteria) that is carried by the brown dog tick. Because the deer tick also carries other diseases, some animals may be at risk for developing more than one tick-borne disease at the same time.

Signs of Anaplasmosis are similar to Ehrlichiosis and include painful joints, diarrhea, fever, and vomiting as well as possible nervous system disorders.

A dog will usually begin to show signs of Anaplasmosis within a couple of weeks after infection and diagnosis will require blood and urine testing, and sometimes other specialized laboratory tests.

Treatment is with oral antibiotics for up to 30 days, depending on how severe the infection may be.

When this disease is quickly treated, most dogs will recover completely, however, subsequent immunity is not guaranteed, which means that a dog may be re-infected if exposed again.

g) Tick Paralysis

Tick paralysis is caused when ticks secrete a toxin that affects the nervous system.

Affected dogs show signs of weakness and limpness approximately one week after being first bitten by ticks.

Symptoms usual begin with a change in pitch of the dog's usual bark, which will become softer, and weakness in the rear legs that eventually involves all four legs, which is then followed by the dog showing difficulty breathing and swallowing.

If the condition is not diagnosed and properly treated, death can occur.

Treatment involves locating and removing the tick and then treating the infected dog with tick anti-serum.

h) Canine Coronavirus

While this highly contagious intestinal disease, which is spread through the feces of contaminated dogs, was first discovered in Germany during 1971 when there was an outbreak in sentry dogs, it is now found worldwide.

This virus can be destroyed by most commonly available disinfectants.

Symptoms include:

- diarrhea
- vomiting
- weight loss or anorexia

While deaths resulting from this disease are rare, and treatment generally requires only medication to relieve the diarrhea, dogs that are more severely affected may require intravenous fluids to combat dehydration. There is a vaccine available, which is usually given to puppies, because they are more susceptible at a young age. This vaccine is also given to show dogs that have a higher risk of exposure to the disease.

i) Leptospirosis

This is a disease that occurs throughout the World that can affect many different kinds of animals, including dogs, and as it is also a zoonotic disease, this means that it can affect humans, too. There is potential for both dogs and humans to die from this disease.

The disease is always present in the environment, which makes it easy for any dog to pick up. This is because it is found in many common animals, such as rats, and wildlife, as well as domestic livestock.

Veterinarians generally see more cases of Leptospirosis in the late summer and fall, which is probably because that is when more pets and wildlife are out and about.

More cases also occur after heavy rain falls.

The disease is most common in mild or tropical climates around the World, and in the US or Canada, it is more common in states or provinces that receive heavy rainfall.

The good news is that you can protect your dog from leptospirosis by vaccination, and while puppies are not routinely vaccinated against leptospirosis because chances of contracting the disease depends upon the lifestyle of the dog as well as the area in which the dog lives, it makes sense to vaccinate against this disease if you and your dog do live in an area considered a hot spot for leptospirosis, so ask your veterinarian.

City rat populations are a major carrier of leptospirosis.

Cold winter conditions lower the risk because the leptospira organisms do not tolerate the freezing and thawing of near-zero temperatures.

They are killed rapidly by drying, but they persist in standing water, dampness, mud and alkaline conditions.

Most of the infected wild animals and domestic animals that spread leptospirosis do not appear ill.

The leptospira take up residence in the kidneys of infected animals, which can include rats, mice, squirrels, skunks, and raccoons and when these animals void urine, they contaminate their environment with living leptospira.

Dogs usually become infected after sniffing urine or by wading, swimming or drinking contaminated water that has infected urine in it, and this is how the disease passes from animal to animal.

As well, the leptospira can also enter through a bite wound or if a dog eats infected material.

5) Additional Vaccinations

According to the place you are living in and the imminent threats faced by people in the area; you might be interested to give additional vaccinations to your pet. Consult your veterinary doctor about the additional vaccinations you can give.

But keep in mind that as a rule of thumb, it is recommended for you not to use any additional vaccinations for your pet till it has reached the age of six months at least. The basic vaccinations given in the form of DHLPP and/or DAPP are sufficient to get it through the initial time period.

6) The Vaccinations Schedule

By and large, your veterinary doctor is in a better state to say how and when you should bring your pet in for vaccinations. Generally, the first one is given at the age of six to eight weeks. The breeder can be held responsible for it.

Then on, the vaccinations are given at an interval of four weeks. After the third shot, the frequency can be tuned down to once every six months or once every year depending on what your veterinary doctor suggests for your canine companion.

Be stringent about the vaccinations schedule. Make sure you follow the guidelines put forth by the veterinary doctor. The responsibility of your pet's health and well-being lies solely with you!

7) De-Worming the Dog

It is an essential practice which ensures the well-being of your Hungarian Vizsla. No matter the hygienic environment you provide to your pet, it is likely to get worms nevertheless. The threat is particularly pronounced during seasonal changes and during travels.

Make sure you take your pet in for inspection periodically. Moreover, take your canine companion in for de-worming after every trip you take to a different state.

The Center for Disease Control suggests the puppy should be taken for de-worming after every two to three weeks. However, some vets suggest a six monthly to yearly schedule. Keep in mind that worms can seriously compromise the health of your pet, so the more frequently you take it for de-working, the better it will work out in the long run!

8) Poison Control

There are quite a few everyday products that can cause poisoning for your pet. Contrary to popular belief, human food and plant-based products are not all perfectly healthy for the canine. Here are a few things you need to be careful about in order to reduce the chances of pet poisoning at home and outside!

a. Knowing Poisonous Foods

While some dogs are smart enough not to want to eat foods that can harm or kill them, other canine companions will eat absolutely anything they can get their teeth on.

As conscientious guardians for our fur friends, it will always be our responsibility to make certain that when we share our homes with a dog, we never leave foods that could be toxic or lethal to them easily within their reach.

While there are many foods that can be toxic to a Hungarian Vizsla, the following alphabetical list contains some of the more common foods that can seriously harm or even kill our dogs including:

Bread Dough: if your dog eats bread dough, their body heat will cause the dough to rise inside the stomach. As the dough expands during the rising process, alcohol is produced.

Dogs that have eaten bread dough may experience stomach bloating, abdominal pain, vomiting, disorientation and depression. Because bread dough can rise to many times its original size, eating only a small amount will cause a problem for any dog.

Broccoli: the toxic ingredient in broccoli is isothiocynate. While it may cause stomach upset, it probably won't be very harmful unless the amount eaten is more than 10% of the dog's total daily diet.

Chocolate: contains theobromine, a chemical that is toxic to dogs in large enough quantities. Chocolate also contains caffeine, which is found in coffee, tea, and certain soft drinks. Different types of chocolate contain different amounts of theobromine and caffeine.

For example, dark chocolate and baking chocolate or cocoa powder contain more of these compounds than milk chocolate does, therefore, a dog would need to eat more milk chocolate in order to become ill.

However, even a few ounces of chocolate can be enough to cause illness or death in a puppy or smaller dog, like the Hungarian

Vizsla, therefore, no amount or type of chocolate should be considered safe for a dog to eat.

Chocolate toxicity can cause vomiting, diarrhea, rapid or irregular heart rate, restlessness, muscle tremors, and seizures. Death can occur within 24 hours of eating.

During many holidays such as Christmas, New Year's, Valentine's, Easter and Halloween, chocolate is often more easily accessible to curious dogs, especially from children who are not so careful with where they might keep their Halloween or Easter egg stash and who are an easy mark for a hungry dog.

In some cases, people unwittingly poison their dogs by offering them chocolate as a treat or leaving chocolate cookies or frosted cake easily within licking distance.

Caffeine: beverages containing caffeine, such as soda, tea, coffee, and chocolate, act as a stimulant and can accelerate your dog's heartbeat to a dangerous level. Dogs eating caffeine have been known to have seizures, some of which are fatal.

Cooked Bones: can be extremely hazardous for a dog because the bones become brittle when cooked which causes them to splinter when the dog chews on them.

The splinters have sharp edges that have been known to become stuck in the teeth, and cause choking when caught in the throat or create a rupture or puncture of the stomach lining or intestinal tract.

Especially dangerous are cooked turkey and chicken legs, ham, pork chop and veal bones. Symptoms of choking include:

- Pale or blue gums
- Gasping open-mouthed breathing
- Pawing at the face
- Slow, shallow breathing

- Falling unconscious with dilated pupils

Grapes and Raisins: can cause acute (sudden) kidney failure in dogs. While it is not known what the toxic agent is in this fruit, clinical signs can occur within 24 hours of eating and include vomiting, diarrhea, and lethargy (tiredness).

Other signs of illness caused from eating grapes or raisins relate to the eventual shutdown of kidney functioning.

Garlic and Onions: contain chemicals that damage red blood cells by rupturing them so that they lose their ability to carry oxygen effectively, which leaves the dog short of oxygen, causing what is called *"hemolytic anemia"*.

Poisoning can occur with a single ingestion of large quantities of garlic or onions or with repeated meals containing small amounts.

Cooking does not reduce the potential toxicity of onions and garlic.

NOTE: fresh, cooked, and/or powdered garlic or onions are commonly found in baby food, which is sometimes given to dogs when they are sick, therefore, be certain to carefully read food labels before feeding to your Hungarian Vizsla.

Macadamia Nuts: are commonly found in candies and chocolates. Although the mechanism of macadamia nut toxicity is not well understood, the clinical signs in dogs having eaten these nuts include depression, weakness, vomiting, tremors, joint pain, and pale gums.

Signs can occur within 12 hours after eating. In some cases, symptoms can resolve themselves without treatment within 24 to 48 hours, however, keeping a close eye on your Hungarian Vizsla will be strongly recommended.

Mushrooms: mushroom poisoning can be fatal if certain species of mushrooms are eaten.

The most commonly reported severely toxic species of mushroom in the US is Amanita phalloides (Death Cap mushroom), which is also quite a common species found in most parts of Britain. Other Amanita species are also toxic.

This deadly mushroom is often found growing in grassy or wooded areas near various deciduous and coniferous trees, which mean that if you're out walking with your Hungarian Vizsla in the woods, they could easily find these mushrooms.

Eating them can cause severe liver disease and neurological disorders. If you suspect your dog has eaten these mushrooms, immediately take them to your veterinarian, as the recommended treatment is to induce vomiting and to give activated charcoal. Further treatment for liver disease may also be necessary.

Pits and Seeds: many seeds and pits found in a variety of fruits, including apples, apricots, cherries, pears and plums, contain cyanogenic glycosides that can cause cyanide poisoning in your Hungarian Vizsla.

The symptoms of cyanide poisoning usually occur within 15-20 minutes to a few hours after eating and symptoms can include initial excitement, followed by rapid respiration rate, salivation, voiding of urine and feces, vomiting, muscle spasm, staggering, and coma before death.

Dogs suffering from cyanide poisoning that live more than 2 hours after onset of symptoms will usually recover.

Raw Salmon or Trout: Salmon Poisoning Disease (SPD) can be a problem for anyone who goes fishing with their dog, or feeds their dog a raw meat diet that includes raw salmon or trout.

When a snail is infected and then is eaten by the fish, as part of the food chain, the dog is exposed when it eats the infected fish.

A sudden onset of symptoms can occur 5-7 days after eating the infected fish. In the acute stages, gastrointestinal symptoms are quite similar to canine parvovirus.

SPD has a mortality rate of up to 90%, can be diagnosed with a fecal sample and is treatable if caught in time.

Prevention is simple, cook all fish before feeding it to your Hungarian Vizsla and immediately see your veterinarian if you suspect that your dog has eaten raw salmon or trout.

Tobacco: all forms of tobacco, including patches, nicotine gum and chewing tobacco can be fatal to dogs if eaten.

Signs of poisoning can appear within an hour and include hyperactivity, salivation, panting, vomiting and diarrhea.

Advanced signs include muscle weakness, twitching, collapse, coma, increased heart rate and eventually cardiac arrest.

Never leave tobacco products within reach of your Hungarian Vizsla, and be careful not to let them pick up discarded cigarette butts when they are young puppies.

If you suspect your dog has eaten any of these, seek immediate veterinary help.

TIP: when your Hungarian Vizsla is a very young puppy, use a double leash, collar and harness arrangement, so that you can still teach them to walk on leash with a Martingale collar around their neck, but can also attach the second leash to their harness so that you can easily lift them over enticing cigarette butts or other toxic garbage they may be trying to eat during your walks.

Tomatoes: contain atropine, which can cause dilated pupils, tremors and irregular heartbeat. The highest concentration of atropine is found in the leaves and stems of tomato plants, next is the unripe (green) tomatoes, followed by the ripe tomato.

Xylitol: is an artificial sweetener found in products such as gum, candy, mints, toothpaste, and mouthwash that is recognized by the National Animal Poison Control Center to be a risk to dogs.

Xylitol is harmful to dogs because it causes a sudden release of insulin in the body that leads to hypoglycemia (low blood sugar). Xylitol can also cause liver damage in dogs.

Within 30 minutes after eating a product containing xylitol, the dog may vomit, be lethargic (tired), and/or be uncoordinated. However, some signs of toxicity can also be delayed for hours or even for a few days. Xylitol toxicity in dogs can be fatal if left untreated.

Please be aware that the above list is just some of the more common foods that can be toxic or fatal to our fur friends and that there are many other foods we should never be feeding our dogs.

If you have one of those dogs who will happily eat anything that looks or smells even slightly like food, be certain to keep these foods far away from your beloved Hungarian Vizsla and you'll help them to live a long and healthy life.

b. Poisonous Plants Inside Your Home

Many common house plants are actually poisonous to our canine companions, and although many dogs simply will ignore house plants, some will attempt to eat anything, especially puppies who want to taste everything in their new world.

More than 700 plant species contain toxins that may harm or be fatal to puppies or dogs, depending on the size of the puppy or dog and how much they may eat. It will be especially important to be aware of household plants that could be toxic when you are sharing your home with a new puppy.

Following is a short list of the more common household plants, what they look like, the different names they are known by, and what symptoms would be apparent if your puppy or dog decides to eat them.

Aloe Plant: (medicine plant or Barbados aloe), is a very common succulent that is toxic to dogs. The toxic agent in this plant is Aloin.

This bitter yellow substance is found in most aloe species and may cause vomiting and/or reddish urine.

Asparagus Fern: (emerald feather, emerald fern, sprengeri fern, plumosa fern, lace fern). The toxic agent in this plant is sapogenin — a steroid found in a variety of plants. Berries of this plant cause vomiting, diarrhea and/or abdominal pain or skin inflammation from repeated exposure.

Corn Plant: (cornstalk plant, dracaena, dragon tree, ribbon plant) is toxic to dogs. Saponin is the offensive chemical compound found in this plant. If the plant is eaten, vomiting (with or without blood), loss of appetite, depression and/or increased salivation can occur.

Cyclamen: (Sowbread) is a pretty, flowering plant that, if eaten, can cause increased salivation, vomiting and diarrhea. If a dog eats a large amount of the plant's tubers, which are usually found below the soil at the root — heart rhythm abnormalities, seizures and even death can occur.

Dieffenbachia: (dumb cane, tropic snow, exotica) contains a chemical that is a poisonous deterrent to animals. If the plant is eaten, oral irritation can occur, especially on the tongue and lips. This irritation can lead to increased salivation, difficulty swallowing and vomiting.

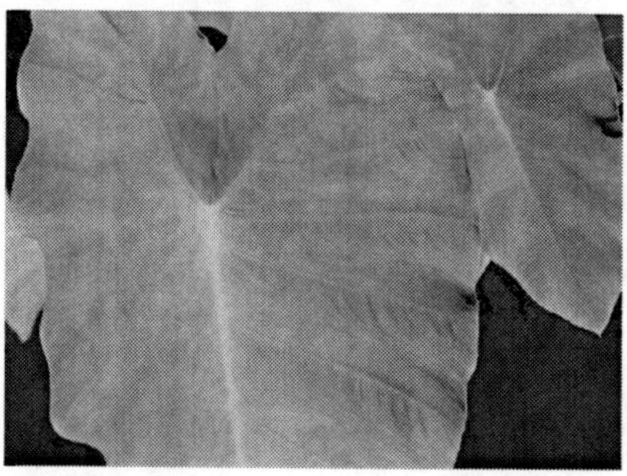

Elephant Ear: (caladium, taro, pai, ape, cape, via, via sori, malanga) contains a chemical similar to that found in dieffenbachia, therefore, a dog's toxic reaction to elephant ear is similar: oral irritation, increased salivation, difficulty swallowing and vomiting.

Heartleaf Philodendron: (horsehead philodendron, cordatum, fiddle leaf, panda plant, split-leaf philodendron, fruit salad plant, red emerald, red princess, saddle leaf), is a common, easy-to-grow houseplant that contains a chemical irritating to the mouth, tongue and lips of dogs. An affected dog may also experience increased salivation, vomiting and difficulty swallowing.

Jade Plant: (baby jade, dwarf rubber plant, jade tree, Chinese rubber plant, Japanese rubber plant, friendship tree). While the toxic property in this plant is unknown, eating it can cause depression, loss of coordination and, although more rare, slow heart rate.

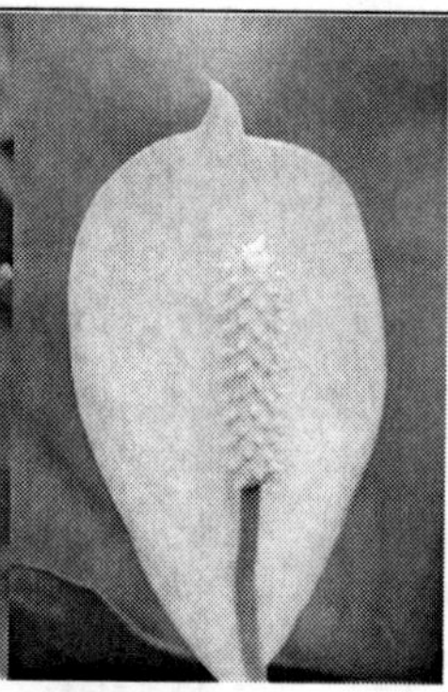

Lilies: some plants of the lily family are toxic to dogs. The peace lily (also known as Mauna Loa) is toxic to dogs. Eating the peace lily or calla lily can cause irritation of the tongue and lips, increased salivation, difficulty swallowing and vomiting.

Satin Pothos: (silk pothos), if eaten by a dog, the plant may cause irritation to the mouth, lips and tongue, while the dog may also experience increased salivation, vomiting and/or difficulty swallowing.

The plants noted above are only a few of the more common household plants, and every conscientious Hungarian Vizsla guardian will want to educate themselves before bringing plants into the home that could be toxic to their canine companions.

c. Poisonous Garden Plants

Please note that there are also many outdoor plants that can be toxic or poisonous to your Hungarian Vizsla, therefore, always check what plants are growing in your garden and if any may be harmful, remove them or make certain that your Hungarian Vizsla puppy or adult dog cannot eat them.

Cornell University, Department of Animal Science lists many different categories of poisonous plants affecting dogs, including house plants, flower garden plants, vegetable garden plants, plants found in swamps or moist areas, plants found in fields, trees and shrubs, plants found in wooded areas, and ornamental plants.

d. Poison Proofing

You can learn about many potentially toxic and poisonous sources both inside and outside your home by visiting the ASPCA Animal Poison Control Center website.

Always keep your veterinarian's emergency number in a place where you can quickly access it, as well as the Emergency Poison Control telephone number, in case you suspect that your dog may have been poisoned.

Knowing what to do if you suspect your dog may have been poisoned and being able to quickly contact the right people could save your Hungarian Vizsla's life.

If you keep toxic cleaning substances (including fertilizers, vermin or snail poisons and vehicle products) in your home or garage, always keep them behind closed doors.

As well, keep any medications where your Hungarian Vizsla can never get to them, and seriously consider eliminating the use of any and all toxic products, for the health of both yourself and your best friend.

e. Symptoms of Poisoning

It is impossible to keep guard over your pet at all times. Naturally, it opens a window of opportunity for your pet to explore around your place. And when it is on this mission, it seldom will respect the boundaries you set for your pet.

On its exploration spree, it can come into contact with or try to ingest those items that can cause poisoning.

Here are some of the symptoms you should look out for that point towards the possibility of poisoning. So even if you were not on guard, you can save your pet from an unfortunate fate by rushing it to the vet in time.

- Abdominal pain.
  Your dog will suddenly begin to whine a lot and when you try to touch its abdomen, you will feel it has become tender.
- Coma.
  Your canine friend will refuse to respond to your orders and will remain in a subconscious state for extended periods of time.
  At this time, you should absolutely take no time to get it to a veterinary doctor as this symbolizes an aggravated stage of poisoning.
- Convulsions.
  Poison can trigger convulsions in your pet.
  Rush it to the vet immediately if your pet begins to convulse all of a sudden.
- Diarrhea.
  Poisons will disrupt its digestive system. So if you see unexplained loose stools, rush to the poison control center or vet immediately.
  Admittedly, this is a much "lighter" version of poisoning. Nevertheless, untimely help can lead it to a horrific fate.
- Drooling.
  It is not much of a problem as most Hungarian Vizsla dogs are

likely to drool. It is normal for quite a few.
However, if you observe your Hungarian Vizsla dog has suddenly started drooling even though it did not do so before, consult a vet.

- Irregular heartbeat.
  Placing a hand on its chest will tell you if its heartbeats are normal or not.
  Like humans, the heartbeats are quite superficial. If you see your Hungarian Vizsla dog exhibiting some of the aforementioned characteristics, immediately roll it over and feel for its heartbeat.
  If it is irregular, you know what you need to do!
- Difficulty breathing.
  It will become evident to you when and if your pet is facing difficulty breathing. It will be making a conscious effort to keep breathing and will refuse to perform any strenuous activities.
  This will become even more evident if you observe it closely for a few minutes while it is lying on the floor.
- Fatigue.
  If your canine companion feels tired, it will automatically show on its face.
  Just keep a close eye on the signs it is giving off and those that are normal to it. Any deviation is almost always an indicator of trouble.
- Swollen limbs.
  Toxins in poisons can cause swelling in its limbs as well as in its internal organs. If it becomes apparent on its limbs, rush it to the emergency services immediately.
  You never know if internal swelling like that on its windpipe might become a major threat to its survival.
- Vomiting.
  Anything that is not tolerated well by its body is likely to be expelled in the form of vomit.
  However, this does not happen every time it tries to ingest poison. If you are sure there is absolutely no other reason why

your pet should begin vomiting all of a sudden, rush it to the vet immediately. A stitch in time saves nine!

If you observe any or all of these symptoms in your pet and you know that they are not normal for it, consult a veterinarian immediately.

If it is too difficult to seek out a veterinarian, look for the nearest poison control center for dogs. In such a situation, time is extremely sensitive to your pet's health. So don't procrastinate and don't take any chances.

Your pet deserves the best so make sure you don't let it down on this!

f. Animal Poison Control Centers

The ASPCA Animal Poison Control Center is staffed 24 hours a day, 365 days a year and is a valuable resource for learning about what plants are toxic and possibly poisonous to your dog.

a) USA Poison Emergency
Call: 1 (888) 426-4435
When calling the Poison Emergency number, a $65. US (£39.42) consultation fee may be applied to your credit card.

b) UK Poison Emergency

Call: 0800-213-6680 - Pet Poison Helpline (payable service)

Call: 0300 1234 999 - RSPCA

www.aspca.org = ASPCA Poison Control.

9) Micro-chipping and Tattooing

Micro-Chipping

A microchip implant is a tiny integrated circuit, approximately twice the size of a large grain of rice, enclosed in glass that is implanted under the skin of a dog (or other animal) with a syringe.

The chip uses passive Radio Frequency Identification (RFID) technology, and is also known as a PIT tag (Passive Integrated Transponder).

The microchip is usually implanted, without anesthetic, into the scruff of a dog's neck by a veterinarian or shelter.

The microchip has no internal power source, which means that they must be read by a scanner or *"interrogator"* which energizes the capacitor in the chip, which then sends radio signals back to the scanner so that the identifying number can be read.

Manufacturers of microchips often donate scanners to animal shelters and veterinarian clinics and hospitals.

While many communities are proposing making micro-chipping of all dogs mandatory, such as N. Ireland, and micro-chipping is a requirements for any dogs traveling to the state of Hawaii, many others are not especially pleased with this idea because they believe it's just more big business for little reward.

For instance, while approximately one quarter of European dogs have a microchip implant, the idea is definitely lacking in popularity in the United States, where only 5% of dogs are micro-chipped.

Even though micro-chipping is used by animal shelters, pounds, animal control officers, breeders and veterinarians, in order to help return a higher percentage of lost canines to their owners, some of the resistance to this idea can be explained by inherent problems with the ability of some organizations to correctly read the implants.

As an example, if the scanner is not tuned to the same frequency as the implanted microchip, it will not be read, which renders the process useless.

Pet microchips are manufactured with different frequencies, including 125 kHz, 128 kHz and 134.2 kHz.

While approximately 98% of the pet microchips in the US use 125 kHz, those in Europe use 134.2 kHz.

In other words, if the facility reading your dog's microchip does not have a compatible scanner, your dog will not be identified and returned to you.

Further, what may turn out to be worse than the scanner incompatibility problem could be the increasing evidence to indicate that microchips may be a probably cause of cancer. As well some microchips will migrate inside the dog's body and while they may start out in the dog's neck, they could end up in their leg or some other body part.

You will have to weigh information known about microchips, including possible cancer risks, and the odds of losing your dog against whether or not a microchip is something you want to have for your Hungarian Vizsla. Whether or not you choose a microchip for your dog, generally the cost ranges between $25 and $50 (£15 and £30) depending on what your veterinarian may charge for this service.

Tattooing

Dogs are tattooed to help identify them in case they are lost or stolen and many dog guardians prefer this safe, simple solution over micro-chipping.

Tattooing does not require locating a scanner that reads the correct frequency and there are no known side effects.

Because a tattoo is visible, it is immediately recognizable and reported when a lost dog is found, which means that tattooing could easily be the most effective means of identification available.

As well, dog thieves are less likely to steal a dog that has a permanent visible form of identification. There are several registries for tattooed dogs, including the National Dog Tattoo Registry in the UK, which has a network of Accredited Tattooists across the UK.

The fee for tattooing and registering a dog for their lifetime is approximately £25.

In the United States, the National Dog Registry (NDR) was founded in 1966 and since then, NDR has supervised, directed, conducted, or overseen the tattooing of more than 6 million animals.

The cost for tattooing a single dog is approximately $10 plus a one-time registration fee of $45.

10) Licensing

Many cities and jurisdictions around the world require the dogs to be licensed.

Usually a dog license is an identifying tag that the dog will be required to wear on their collar. The tag will have an identifying number and a contact number for the registering organization, so that if someone finds a lost dog wearing a tag, the owner of the dog can be contacted.

Most dog tags are only valid for one year, and will need to be renewed annually at the beginning of every New Year, which involves paying a fee, which can vary from jurisdiction to jurisdiction.

From one extreme to the next, owners of dogs living in Beijing, China must pay a licensing fee of $600. (£360), while those living in Great Britain require no fee, because licensing of dogs was abolished in 1987.

Ireland and Northern Ireland both require dogs to be licensed and in Germany dog ownership is taxed, rather than requiring licensing, with higher taxes being paid for breeds of dogs deemed to be "dangerous".

Most US states and municipalities have licensing laws in effect and Canadian, Australian and New Zealand dogs also must be licensed, with the yearly fee approximately $30 to $50 (£18 to £30) depending upon whether the dog has been spayed or neutered.

11) Pet Insurance

Pet guardians commonly ask themselves, when considering medical insurance for their dog, whether they can afford not to have it.

On the one hand, in light of all the new treatments and medications that are now available for our dogs which usually come with a very high price tag, an increasing number of guardians have decided to add pet insurance to their list of monthly expenses. On the other hand, some humans believe that placing money into a savings account, in case unforeseen medical treatments are required, makes more sense.

Pet insurance coverage can cost anywhere from $2,000 to $6,000 USD (£1201 to £3604) over an average lifespan of a dog, and unless your dog is involved in a serious accident, or contracts a life-threatening disease, you may never need to pay out that much for treatment.

Whether you decide to start a savings account for your Hungarian Vizsla so that you will always have funds available for unforeseen health issues, or you decide to buy a health insurance plan, most dog lovers will go to any lengths to save the life of their beloved companions.

Having access to advanced technological tools and procedures means that our dogs are now being offered treatment options that were once only reserved for humans.

Now, some canine conditions that were once considered fatal, are being treated at considerable costs ranging anywhere between $1,000 and $5,000 (£597 and £2,986) and more. However, even in the face of rapidly increasing costs of caring for our dogs, owners purchasing pet insurance remain a small minority.

In an effort to increase the numbers of people buying pet insurance, insurers have teamed with the American Kennel Club and Petco Animal Supplies to offer the insurance, and more than 1,600 companies, such as Office Depot and Google, offer pet insurance coverage to their employees as an optional employee benefit. Even though you might believe that pet insurance will be your savior anytime your dog needs a trip to the vet's office, you really need to be careful when considering an insurance plan, because there are many policies that contain small print excluding certain ages, hereditary or chronic conditions.

Unfortunately, most people don't consider pet insurance when their pets are healthy because buying pet insurance means playing the odds, and unless your dog becomes seriously ill, you end up paying for something that may never happen.

However, just like automobile insurance, you can't buy it after you've had that accident. Therefore, since many of us, in today's uncertain economy, may be hard pressed to pay a high veterinarian bill, generally speaking, the alternative of paying monthly pet insurance premiums will provide peace of mind and improved veterinarian care for our best friends.

Shop around, because as with all insurance policies, pet insurance policies will vary greatly between companies and the only way to know for certain exactly what sort of coverage you are buying is to be holding a copy of that policy in your hand so that you can clearly read what will and what will not be covered. Don't forget to carefully read the fine print to avoid any nasty surprises, because the time to discover that a certain procedure will not be covered is not when you are in the middle of filing a claim.

Before Purchasing a Policy

- There are several considerations to be aware of before choosing to purchase a pet insurance policy, including: Is your dog required to undergo a physical exam?
- Is there a waiting period before the policy becomes active?
- What percentage of the bill does the insurance company pay — after the deductible?
- Are payments limited or capped in any way?
- Are there co-pays (cost to you up front)?
- Does the plan cover pre-existing conditions?
- Does the plan cover chronic or recurring medical problems?
- Can you choose any vet or animal hospital to treat your pet?
- Are prescription medications covered?
- Are you covered when travelling with your pet?
- Does the policy pay if your pet is being treated and then dies?

When you love your dog and worry that you may not have the funds to cover an emergency medical situation that could unexpectedly cost thousands, the right pet insurance policy will provide both peace of mind and better health care for your beloved fur friend.

Chapter 14: Financial Aspects

As far as the cost of upkeep is concerned, the Hungarian Vizsla is a fairly reasonable breed. From the initial cost of acquisition to the periodic cost of maintenance and otherwise; the breed is more or less affordable for all. What really makes the difference between a successful and an unsuccessful relationship is this; how well are you able to provide for your dog's elaborate needs?!

Here are some of the expenses you will incur on a regular basis. These do not include the initial cost of acquisition. The topic has been covered adequately in the previous pages. Make sure you build a monthly expense schedule for your puppy and stick with it; it will prevent you from going bankrupt!

In some cases, you will come across Hungarian Vizsla puppies being sold for a premium price – sometimes considerably more than the cost of other similar dogs. This is because for this breed, pedigree or purebred is the first preference. A pedigree is less likely to develop health problems and hence is likely to live happier and longer.

Even so, the premium price is not a necessity. You can find perfectly healthy Hungarian Vizslas for much lower cost. It all depends on you and your resources. Make sure you invite other dog owners to share their views on the topic; it will help you make a positive decision for the long term benefit of both parties!

1) Food

As far as the Hungarian Vizsla's food is concerned, it is a continuous expense that you will incur throughout the life of your pet.

The thing about petting Hungarian Vizsla is this; in order to keep them healthy, fit and athletic, you need to feed them high quality premium dog food. However, this does not necessarily mean you will end up overspending your resources!

Premium dog foods are high quality foods designed with the idea of providing your pet with the right combination of nutrients upfront.

If you've observed closely, you will find that you need to feed fewer and smaller servings of premium dog food when contrasted against economy foods. This is because economy foods need to be served in larger quantities in order to deliver the same amount of nutrients as delivered by smaller quantities of premium dog food.

In the long run, premium dog foods can actually help you save a lot. On average, you'll be required to spend somewhere between $14 and $18 per week to satisfy your pet's hunger. In the UK, this cost may be between £4 and £8. When it comes to economy food, the cost will be higher because you'll need to use more bags of dog food in a given period as compared with premium dog foods.

This does not include the cost of treats. Especially during the training phase, you'll need to invest heavily in treats. This can cost you up to $20 per bag. And depending on the amount of treats you give to your pet on a daily basis, this can add up to a sizeable value.

For older Hungarian Vizsla pets and for those with known medical problems, there will be an additional cost of supplements or medicines. This can range between $10 and $300 per bottle/box. Supplements are an effective way of overcoming nutritional gaps where it is not possible to cover up with diet!

On the whole, the cost of your dog's food on a monthly basis can amount between $100 and $300. This is the biggest cost factor you'll be incurring throughout the dog ownership phase. And then there will be other expenses. You need to be mentally prepared for this kind of an expense beforehand to ensure a happy and healthy transition into the relationship.

2) Accessories

Your pet needs a few essential accessories just like you do! This would include things like a travel crate, dog toys, grooming sets and other similar accessories. These items can incur a significant initial cost. However, usually these items are purchased for long term use and hence their cost is justified!

A travel crate can cost anywhere between $100 to $300 depending on the quality and size of the crate. If you are purchasing a bigger crate to accommodate your Hungarian Vizsla as it grows up, you wouldn't need to buy it again and again. A single travel crate can be useful for you for the entire duration of your association!

Don't forget the collars and leashes for your pet! They can cost you anywhere between $10 and $200 depending on the quality and style of items that you purchase. Essentially the basic purpose of all items will be the same. It will just differ in the manner of its looks and (sometimes) in added utility features.

The grooming kit can take up a good part of your budget. But as with previous options, a wise investment can serve its purpose throughout the lifetime of your pet. Nail clippers and trimmers cost up to $60. It is worth investing in such an equipment to keep yourself and your property safe from scratches etc.

You'll need a brush in order to massage your Hungarian Vizsla's coat. The one with organic hair works best. Such a comb may cost you up to $50. But the organic nature of the brush will ensure it does not emit any kind of toxins that may affect the health of your pet.

Puppy wipes and puppy pee pads can cost a minimum of $20. The periodic cost largely depends on the frequency of usage. If you are using it more frequently, you'll be incurring a higher cost. Generally, puppy pee pads come in handy during the initial training phase; over time, you'll be able to overcome this expense altogether.

On the whole, your pet can incur up to $150 in grooming costs. But it is a one-time expenditure – you'll be using these equipments more or less the same way throughout your life!

Alternatively, you can choose to take your pet to dog parlors. The services are usually much more expensive than this. Every parlor visit can cost you up to $60. In the long run (since we are talking about no less than 10 years' of association), this can amount up to several thousand!

Last but not the least; you need dog toys to entertain your Hungarian Vizsla at times when you are not around. The dog toys are generally quite affordable and carefully constructed to make sure they do not pose as a threat to it. A dog toy's prices may start from $15 and can range up to several hundred depending on the quality and style of dog toys you choose for your pet!

If you are planning your expenses intelligently, you'll be able to purchase such products that last a lifetime. Over such a time period, the returns are much higher than the initial investment!

3) The Vet

When it comes to the Hungarian Vizsla, the medical expenses are more likely to be significant. This is because this particular breed is prone to a number of health problems ranging from hereditary problems to short term problems.

Once inflicted with a particular disease, it will be extremely difficult to reverse the condition. In most cases, the diseases are incurable once they have progressed. Therefore timely diagnosis is the key to its health and well-being.

Choosing the right veterinary doctor should be one of your prime most concerns even before you head out to hunt for a reliable breeder. Some of the tips to choose the right breeder are already mentioned in here. Once you've selected the right vet, make sure you consult him/her regularly for all your pet-related concerns.

The general rule of thumb says you need to take your pet to the veterinary doctor at least once every year. However, if your pet doesn't seem to be in a very good shape, a semi-annual or quarterly visit may be in order. Whatever you decide about the frequency, make sure you stick to the schedule religiously.

A visit to the vet often costs about $100 to $150 per visit. The prices may vary according to different locations and experts. In some cases, the costs of tests are included in the consultation fee to make it more reasonable. You'll need to do your research in order to figure out the option which suits you the best.

For a sick dog, the costs will be inevitably high. So if you are planning to take in a rescue dog, make sure you have an idea about the costs beforehand.

Apart from this, if you choose to spay or neuter your pet, it will incur a one-time cost. Spaying costs about $170 to $240. Neutering can cost you about $120 to $175. It depends largely on the locality and experience of your veterinary doctor! Generally, the long term gains of these procedures significantly surpass the immediate cost of the treatment!

4) Dog Training

This brings us to one of the most important aspects of petting a Hungarian Vizsla. You will need to invest in training your puppy dog throughout the period of its life. Consistent training is a must if you are hoping to groom a well-disciplined pet.

As with the veterinary doctor, the locality and experience of the dog trainer/ training institute will determine how much it will cost you to enroll your pet in a course. Different courses may have different durations and number of visits. The prices will vary accordingly.

For the most part, single sessions will be considerably inexpensive. A single session course may cost you about $10 and $15 depending on the number of hours required. It might a little higher if it is an all day course.

Some courses may stretch over a period of four to six weeks. These courses may cost you about $150 to $250. Such courses will require you to attend the sessions at specific times during the week. Make sure you are there for every session. Rest assured, each session will be a new experience for your pet and if you miss out on any particular session, it will decrease the overall effectiveness of the training course!

There are several different dog training courses available differentiated according to the complexity level and age of your dog. There will be a course for every puppy/dog. You'll just need to look around a little in order to figure out which one is an absolute must-have for your pet!

Make sure you consult with a dog expert to know which kinds of training courses are needed. Feel free to share your experiences and opinions. Get your puppy enrolled in the sessions in a timely manner in order to obtain greater gains from your investment.

Obedience training, respect training and housebreaking training are some of the essentials you need to get for your pet. The rest depends on your individual situations.

5) Miscellaneous Expenses

This isn't all. There might be a few other expenses here and there that you'll need to make in order to provide your pet with a good quality life. For instance, if you plan to put certain installations in place in order to prevent your puppy from transgressing limits, it will essentially come from your pocket! You wouldn't need to make the same expense time and again but it will essentially be a part of your pet's budget!

Moreover, property damage is next to inevitable. There will surely be some kind of property damage, especially during the training period. This kind of expense comes in the form of replacement (of damaged goods). Over time, however, you'll be able to overcome the initial tantrums quite effectively.

It is a big decision if you are bringing a pet to your house. The first year will be the hardest but it will eventually become easier for both the parties. Make sure you are not making a hasty decision; you don't want to regret bringing it in if you cannot afford it in the first place!

There will be a few more expenses here and there. Keep an additional hundred or two aside for your pet. When the time comes, it will automatically start making sense why petting a dog is not an easy choice.

The estimates given in here are just to give you an idea about what petting a Hungarian Vizsla may mean to you. For the dog, it is all about love – the more it gets from you, the more it will give to you! Hungarian Vizslas can be pretty sticky and bothersome, especially if you are not used to their style of affection.

Keeping in mind the information you've received from this book, ask yourself once again; are you willing to pet a Hungarian Vizsla? If you are up for the challenge, we wish you all the best with all your future endeavors!

Chapter 15: General Tips, Tricks and Guidelines

Here are a few guidelines for taking care of a canine companion in general. Regardless of the breed that you own, you can care for your canine companion in a better way by keeping in mind the following things.

1) Helping the Puppy Transition

The impending loss of a beloved dog is one of the most painfully difficult and emotionally devastating experiences a canine guardian will ever have to face.

For the sake of our faithful companions, because we do not want to prolong their suffering, we humans will have to do our best to look at our dog's situation practically, rather than emotionally, so that we can make the best decision for them.

They may be suffering from extreme old age and the inability to even walk outside to relieve themselves, and thus having to deal with the indignity of regularly soiling their sleeping area, they may have been diagnosed with an incurable illness that is causing them much pain, or they may have been seriously injured.

Whatever the reason for a canine's suffering, it will be up to their human guardian to calmly guide the end-of-life experience so that any further discomfort and distress can be minimized.

What to Do If You Are Uncertain?

In circumstances where it is not entirely clear how much a dog is suffering, it will be helpful to pay close attention to your Hungarian Vizsla dog's behavior and keep a daily log or record so that you can know for certain how much of their day is difficult and painful for them, and how much is not.

When you keep a daily log, it will be easier to decide if the dog's quality of life has become so poor that it makes better sense to offer them the gift of peacefully going to sleep.

During this time of uncertainty, it will also be very important to discuss with your veterinarian what signs of suffering may be associated with the dog's particular disease or condition, so that you know what to look for.

Often a dog may still continue to eat or drink despite being upset, having difficulty breathing, excessively panting, being disoriented or in much pain, and as their caring guardians, we will have to weigh their love of eating against how much they are really suffering in all other aspects of their life.

Obviously, if a canine guardian can clearly see that their beloved companion is suffering throughout their days and nights, it will make sense to help humanely end their suffering by planning a euthanasia procedure.

We humans are often tempted to delay the inevitable moment of euthanasia, because we love our dogs so much and cannot bear the anticipation of the intense grief we know will overwhelm us when we must say our final goodbyes to our beloved fur friend.

Unfortunately, we may regret that we allowed our dog to suffer too long, and could find ourselves wishing that if only we humans had the same option, to peacefully let go, when we find ourselves in such a stage in our own lives.

2) Euthanasia – What, Why and How?

Every veterinarian will have received special training to help provide all incurably ill, injured or aged pets that have come to the end of their natural lives with a humane and gentle death, through a process called *"euthanasia"*.

When the time comes, euthanasia, or putting a dog *"to sleep"*, will usually be a two-step process.

First, the veterinarian will inject the dog with a sedative to make them sleepy, calm and comfortable.

Second, the veterinarian will inject a special drug that will peacefully stop their heart.

These drugs work in such a way that the dog will not experience any awareness whatsoever that their life is ending. What they will experience is very much like what we humans experience when falling asleep under anesthesia during a surgical procedure.

Once the second stage drug has been injected, the entire process takes about 10 to 20 seconds, at which time the veterinarian will then check to make certain that the dog's heart has stopped.

There is no suffering with this process, which is a very gentle and humane way to end a dog's suffering and allow them to peacefully pass on.

3) Where Most Dog/Puppy Owners Go Wrong

Here are some of the common mistakes made by people while petting their canine companions.

Make sure you are not one of them as this can seriously disrupt your relationship with your Hungarian Vizsla dog at some point in time or the other!

a. Experimentation

First and foremost, you should not experiment with your pet, especially in matters pertaining to its health.

Self-medication is the last thing you should do even if your pet seems to have developed a problem that had occurred previously. You might be inclined to do so in order to save some costs but do keep in mind the dog doesn't respond to medication in the same way as humans.

If and when your plan backfires, the results will be even more drastic!

b. Sleeping in Your Bed

As stressed on multiple occasions, you should never let the canine sleep with you in your bed. Many of us humans make the mistake of allowing a crying puppy to sleep in their bed, and while this may help to calm and comfort a new puppy, it will set a dangerous precedent that can result in behavioral problems later in their life.

As much as it may pull on your heart strings to hear your new Hungarian Vizsla puppy crying the first couple of nights in their kennel, a little tough love at the beginning will keep them safe while helping them to learn to both love and respect you as their leader.

c. Playing Too Hard or Too Long

Many humans play too hard or allow their children to play too long or too roughly with a young puppy.

You need to remember that a young puppy tires very easily and especially during the critical growing phases of their young life, they need their rest.

d. Hand Play

Always discourage your Hungarian Vizsla puppy from chewing or biting your hands, or any part of your body for that matter.

If you allow them to do this when they are puppies, they will want to continue to do so when they have strong jaws and adult teeth and this is not acceptable behavior for any breed of dog.

Do not get into the habit of playing the "hand" game, where you rough up the puppy and slide them across the floor with your hands, because this will teach your puppy that your hands are playthings.

When your puppy is teething, they will naturally want to chew on everything within reach, and this will include you. As cute as you might think it is, this is not an acceptable behavior and you need to gently, but firmly, discourage the habit.

A light flick with a finger on the end of a puppy nose, combined with a firm "NO" when they are trying to bite human fingers will discourage them from this activity.

e. Extraordinary Creation

You should not consider it as an extraordinary being of any sort. It cannot take care of itself, cannot recognize what may be lethal for it and definitely cannot be expected to adapt or adjust to different settings.

It is not human, and you being its owner are responsible for keeping it healthy. Don't be negligent about your pet's needs – you never know when you might end up harming your own pal.

f. Being Too Distracted

If you have too many distractions to keep you busy through days or nights, are planning to have a child of your own, are one of the laid back types or simply cannot devote time and attention to your pet for whatever reason, it is best to stay away from such a commitment.

Hungarian Vizsla dogs demand more effort as compared to other breeds. If you cannot keep up with its pace, well then don't get involved!

g. No Need for Training

Besides this, never be misled into believing your Hungarian Vizsla dog is naturally well-behaved or does not need training because it seems to be doing very well without it.

Hungarian Vizsla dogs learn quickly and will therefore follow your orders easily. However, it wouldn't be long before its internal state of crisis will get into the way of obedience.

Start training the Hungarian Vizsla dog as early as possible to make sure that unfortunate occurrences can be kept to a bare minimum.

The more you delay training for your Hungarian Vizsla dog, the more stubborn and irresponsive it will become. So it is in your best interest not to procrastinate this duty.

h. Inconsistent Orders

On the same note, make sure you (and your family) use consistent words for specific actions.

Your Hungarian Vizsla is not a human and will therefore become extremely confused if you use the same word and expect it to act differently.

Even if it is impulsively and linguistically right, the same cannot be said for your pet's understanding.

Consider this for example; if you want it to sit on the floor, you say "down" and when your spouse wants it off the sofa, they say "down". It will become worse when your kid says "down" to get the Hungarian Vizsla dog down a flight of stairs.

Linguistically, the word is used correctly in all three situations. But it is creating confusion in the mind of the Hungarian Vizsla about what the owner(s) wants.

It is best to use separate words for different actions and then reinforce this definition to make sure your Hungarian Vizsla dog respond well.

i. Not Using Enough Treats

It is recommended to use treats often, especially during the training phase. It is easily the best way to reinforce actions and responses.

So whenever your pet follows your orders or responds to the most recent training class, treat it with some snacks. It will know when it is being praised and will therefore respond to make you happy.

j. Leaving It off the Leash

Never try to leave your Hungarian Vizsla dog off the leash until and unless you are absolutely sure it is well disciplined.

Although it is encouraged to conduct your training sessions in public areas or in places where numerous distractions exist, make sure you do so once your pet has understood the basics.

Training amidst distractions makes sure your pet responds to your orders in similar situations.

But if you leave it off the leash before training sessions take effect, it is more likely to wander off to restricted territories, bite a few people or animals and get you into a lot of trouble that could have been avoided if you kept the leash intact!

k. Leaving it Unattended

Lastly and most importantly, don't let your pet get lonely or leave it unsupervised for long time periods.

It is a disastrous combination which can result in all sorts of damage – to your property as well as your pet. A lonely

Hungarian Vizsla is likely to experiment with different objects within the house. Such activities are not always uneventful.

Also, don't leave it unsupervised in a place where known threats exist. For instance, don't keep it locked in the car or leave it around a park without supervision. Such negligence may end up inflicting irreversible pain to your pet.

l. Expecting too much!

Don't expect too much from your pet in too little time. Patience and perseverance is the key to success. Let your Hungarian Vizsla dog settle in and absorb your rules – it will eventually get there. Haste can only make matters worse for you as well as for your newfound pet!

4) Caring for Aged Dogs

m Caring for an aging dog is slightly different from caring for a puppy. Their demands and needs are infinitely different. It is common to come across one if you are involved in rescuing the Hungarian Vizsla breed. Here are some of the things you need to keep in mind while handling aged Hungarian Vizsla dogs.

Aged Hungarian Vizsla dogs, especially if they come from battered homes, are likely to have several health issues. Make sure you keep these in mind while preparing their meals and activities.

It is advised not to serve them any hard foods or bones that can damage their gums. Also, keep the oil content in foods low so that digestive issues can be kept to a minimum.

On this note, keep in mind that some of the health problems faced by your Hungarian Vizsla dog are likely to come naturally with age. There is no way to delay or eliminate these.

For instance, most aged dogs will experience reduced hearing and sight. Learn to differentiate between imminent dangers and the natural course of life.

Your veterinary doctor is more skilled to tell you about the different signs likely to be exhibited by your pet. However, it pays to consider anything out of the ordinary as a potential threat for your pet's well-being!

Aged Hungarian Vizsla dogs are not likely to be as energetic as young ones. Plan their activities in a placid manner.

Remember to take them out for walks and other activities as it helps prevent the arthritis from becoming a major problem.

Select a peaceful space in your house where they can rest through the day. You can take them for rides but beware of their stress urinary incontinence.

Don't forget the annual checkups. Better still increase its frequency to semi-annually.

As far as the vaccinations are concerned, ask your veterinary doctor if it is advisable to tune down the frequency to once every three years.

Besides this, you might need to use some vitamins and supplements to counter failing health. The rest all should be fine.

Conclusion

The Hungarian Vizsla is a unique Velcro breed that doesn't have a lot of hair but exhibits an upright and attractive personality. Generally, the breed is extremely attractive from every aspect. If you have what it takes to pet a Hungarian Vizsla, rest assured it will a journey you will cherish through the rest of your life!

This book aims to introduce you to this amazing breed – its needs, likes, dislikes and everything else that you need to know in order to pet the Hungarian Vizsla. Besides this, it aims to give you an insight about the origin of this breed to help you understand what its natural habitat is. This information will not only help you make the right petting decision but also help you care for your pet in the right way.

The Hungarian Vizsla dogs make remarkable companions though you need to be extra careful about where you are getting your pet from. Seeing that the breed is prone to a number of genetic problems, you need one that is pedigree in order to prevent an untimely lapse. The rest should be fine.

It is recommended for you to think and reconsider your decision to purchase a Hungarian Vizsla before you head out to buy one. But once you buy one, make sure you are being a responsible owner and dog enthusiast by caring for its needs rightfully.

We wish you all the best for your petting experience!